TROUT
FISHING
IN
NEW ENGLAND

TROUT
FISHING
IN
NEW ENGLAND

HAROLD F. BLAISDELL

STONE WALL PRESS

Second Printing 1974
Third Printing 1977

ISBN 0-913276-02-2

Books by Harold F. Blaisdell:

TRICKS THAT TAKE FISH

THE PHILOSOPHICAL FISHERMAN

CONTENTS

ACKNOWLEDGMENTS

Sincere thanks are expressed for the technical assistance and photographs so kindly furnished by the following individuals, agencies and manufacturing concerns: Mr. Baird Hall of The Orvis Company, Harrison-Hoge Industries, Inc., Mr. "Letty" Kreh, Outdoor Writer and Photographer, Maine Fish and Game Department, Mr. Leon L. Martuch of Scientific Anglers, Inc., Pflueger, and the Vermont Fish and Game Service. In addition, thanks are due the many companions on streams and lakes from whom I have learned a great deal in my half-century of trout fishing.

1973   Harold F. Blaisdell

INTRODUCTION

Back in the days when Curt Gowdy was broadcasting the games of the Boston Red Sox, the now famous sportscaster was often moved to refer to baseball as "a game of inches." The description is apt for it hints of the subtle distinctions and characteristics which place baseball in a one-only category in the field of competetive athletics.

By much the same token, New England trout fishing can be described as a game of tiny touches and delicate refinements. Both baseball and trout fishing have their grassroots in the soil of broad and basic techniques, but the difference between success and failure in both activities is often determined by minute dabs of inspirational strategy, applied with just the right touch at just the right moment.

This book will attempt to deal with the broad techniques of eastern trout fishing, while honoring the conviction that the really fine points of the game are learned only from experience. There is virtue in this circumstance, however, for trout fishing triumphs achieved through independent efforts bring gratifications which can be realized in no other way.

Unfortunately, the urban trout fishing aspirant does not have the time and opportunity to achieve all by trial and error. His nearest trout stream may be hours away, and his days that are free for fishing are likely to be severely limited.

The author's main intent is to give such beginners, and perhaps anglers of intermediate experience, a helping hand. The sooner they can get into the thick of things, the sooner they can start enjoying the quiet thrills and satisfactions of trout fishing.

This does not seem to be an overly ambitious goal, for the trout fisherman need only take a few trout to make his day a success and a source of enjoyment. It is the writer's hope that if this book concerns itself with basic fundamentals, it can induce the modest amount of skill which this equally modest goal requires, and can thus be of service to those who are long on trout fishing enthusiasm but short on experience and opportunity.

As for the subtle touches which denote the journeyman trout fisherman, the author has stockpiled his personal repertoire, such as it may be, from nearly 50 years of trout fishing. While he knows better than to think that he can pass on directly these gleanings from long experience, they will tinge what he has to say and perhaps a bit here and there hopefully will rub off on the reader to his benefit.

Since what follows will deal with *eastern* trout fishing as a separate phase of the sport, perhaps a word of explanation concerning that point is in order. To the author, eastern trout fishing is, indeed, a distinct category of the game, the distinction lying in that it is trout fishing stripped of all excesses.

The New England fisherman cannot realistically set his sights on trophy trout, for competition precludes their existence in all but rare exceptions. He will wade few broad, brawling rivers, brave few dangers and endure few hardships. For the most part, his streams will be quiet, gentle and inviting, handily bordered by highways and thus easily approached.

Oddly enough, despite heavy fishing pressure and the encroachment of urbanization, trout are there—often in considerably greater numbers than seems reasonable to expect. Their general run will be of modest size, but what they may lack in bulk they more than make up in sophistication. These are trout with defensive sensitivities which have evolved as many generations of forebearers have stood off the best efforts of generations of fishermen. The eastern trout fisherman takes his position in the ranks of the latter with the full knowledge that in his rather unpretentious adversary he will meet more than his match.

The angler who accepts this quiet challenge, in its context of gentle surroundings and modest goals, eventually realizes what is perhaps the ultimate among all the charms of trout fishing. If this book can aid and abet the search for these unique delights, it will have served its intended purpose.

TROUT
FISHING
IN
NEW ENGLAND

1

THE QUARRY

If there is a common reason for defeat and humiliation, it is probably the sad habit of underestimating the strength and resources of the enemy and overestimating those of our own.

In trout fishing, it is tempting to visualize trout as a relatively low order of life with correspondingly few resources from which to fashion their defenses. It is equally tempting to assume that the difference in intellect between trout and man gives man an overwhelming advantage in the matter of bamboozling the trout into gulping a hook disguised as food. *Hah!*

During the year 1971, trout fishermen who frequented the famous Battenkill in southwestern Vermont, registered a protest with the Vermont Fish and Game Commission. They could catch only small trout they complained, thus proving beyond a shadow of a doubt that only small trout existed in the 'Kill. It was high time, they insisted, that the Commission get busy and do something about it.

For those who may not know, the Battenkill is one of the most famous trout streams in New England. Moreover, the Orvis Company, producers of world renowned trout fishing rods and tackle, is situated almost on the Battenkill's banks in Manchester. The river thus forms an ideal testing ground for Orvis tackle and for some of the world's best anglers who are attracted to the scene by both the fount of custom tackle and the stream itself.

*Fifteen inch brown trout taken during the Battenkill shocking.
The Vermont Sportsman.*

In other words, the Battenkill gets pounded not only by hayshakers like me, but by many from the elite of the angling world. And when *they* can take only tiny fish, somebody, indeed, had better do something!

The Commission responded by sending a crew to "shock" the Battenkill. Electrical shocking is a standard method of estimating trout populations. It involves discharging an electrical current into a stream, powerful enough to stun trout long enough for netting and counting.

The results in this instance constituted no ringing endorsement of human superiority or perception. In almost every run and pool, each of which had been pounded to little avail by some of the trout fishing world's best arms and rods, the probing electrical jolt brought to the surface an embarrassing superabundance of large trout, the very trout which so many experts (?) had vindictively claimed to be lacking!

I am sure that it was with smug satisfaction that the Fish and Game Commission succinctly issued its finding: The trouble was not the quality of the fishing, but the quality of the fishermen!

Baird Hall, editor of the always interesting *Orvis Newsletter,* is an ardent and skillful trout fisherman. Unlike many, however, he entertains no illusions concerning human superiority over trout, particularly with respect to the trout of the Battenkill. During a recent visit to his home he told me of a personal experience illustrative of the latter's supersensitivity.

He and a friend, he told me, spotted a pair of fish rising steadily in a run just downstream from a bridge which crosses the 'Kill. From the bridge, Baird was able to observe the fish clearly and to direct his friend's casts accordingly.

"There were two browns," Baird said, "a real dandy and one smaller. They were holding steady against the current and tipping up for mayflies as casually as kids finger popcorn from paper bags.

"I helped my friend get the range with false casts, and when he finally let it go his dry fly fell flawlessly above the bigger fish.

"I'm sure the float looked just as perfect to my friend," Baird continued, "but from the bridge I could detect just the hint of drag as the fly came over the trout. No sooner did it come within their view than *both* trout went down as though somebody had heaved in a brick. The larger trout never did reappear, and it was fully twenty minutes before the smaller fish resumed feeding.

"When my friend made a try for him," Baird concluded, "it was the same story all over again."

Such defensive sensitivity on the part of the trout is not the product of intelligence, of course, but as far as the fisherman is concerned, it might as well be. When it reaches the ultimate, as it has among the trout of the

3

Brook trout.
Vermont Fish & Game Department.

A Vermont brown trout on fall spawning run negotiates falls on Black River in Coventry.
Vermont Fish & Game Department.

Battenkill, it is all but impossible to cope with within the measures accepted as honorable by the trout fishing fraternity.

Fortunately, trout are not always, and not everywhere, so. During a sudden rise in water, the most sophisticated brown trout may become a pushover for a nightcrawler. During heavy hatches of mayflies, when the very conditions which have inspired the hatch have caused trout metabolism to soar, trout which will soon become shy and much harder to take are temporarily easy pickings for the dry fly fisherman.

Between the two extremes lies the general nature of our quarry, and it will be well to examine his habits and characteristics in detail. Then, from a position of basic understanding, we can attempt his undoing by attacking where his defenses seem weakest.

Experts with the passion for fine distinctions like to point out that the brook trout and the lake trout are *chars* while the brown trout and rainbow trout are truly *trout*. So far as the fisherman is concerned, this is making much of almost nothing. Although all trout are not chars, all chars *are* trout; so, for our purpose, trout is properly an all-inclusive term and is used here as such.

Common to New England ponds, lakes and streams nowadays are brook trout, rainbow trout, brown trout and lake trout. (The lake trout's habits are quite different from those of the other three, and the laker will be discussed in a separate chapter.)

The brook trout is the only one of the remaining three that is truly native to New England. The rainbow, a native of the West Coast, is here as a result of import and stocking as is the brown trout, originally a native of European waters.

Some trout fishermen profess to preferences, the brookie generally winning out as the sentimental favorite. This is a point unworthy of our consideration, for all three species require the fisherman's best efforts and are thus equally deserving of his admiration and respect.

What does matter to us are any differences in habit which may set the species apart sufficiently to require modifications of angling techniques. Despite what you may have heard or read, the differences are so slight that they may be all but ignored, standard techniques working equally well on all three save for a few minor exceptions which follow.

All trout feed at night to a certain extent, but the larger browns are demonstrably more nocturnal. Under cover of darkness they become surprisingly bold and democratic in taste. This change can be exploited by fishing for them after dark with large flies that would be prohibitive during the day.

6

In general, browns tend to be the hardest of all trout to take, particularly after they exceed a foot in length. However, their capture is seldom a matter of devising new lures or methods but of attaining near perfection in the execution of standard techniques.

Browns and brookies are fall spawners, while rainbows normally spawn in the spring. (It should be noted as an exception that some hatchery reared rainbows are fall spawners.) In streams which hold brookies and/or browns, the good fishing for them tends to move toward the headwaters as the season approaches fall and the fish migrate upstream toward spawning sites. This circumstance can be used to increasingly good advantage nowadays, for most states are becoming increasingly liberal in extending legal seasons.

Conversely, at the beginning of the season, hefty rainbows are often taken in tributary streams in April and May as they carry out their spawning runs.

Two examples of such species oriented vulnerability will suffice.

The first is a run of large rainbows in Vermont's Willoughby River which attracts hundreds of early season anglers from many of the eastern states. The fish begin moving into the river from Lake Memphremagog in April and continue well into May, the peak of the run depending on yearly differences in conditions. Legal fishing begins April 15, usually when banks are knee-deep with snow, and with the opening, hordes of eager fishermen descend on the tiny village of Orleans through which the Willoughby flows.

When the run is on in earnest, many beautiful rainbows are caught on mesh bags of roe, on sponge imitations thereof, on mesh bags of tapioca and on nightcrawlers. Fishermen who stick to artificial lures are almost always disappointed. The whole affair has great appeal for many, while its Roman Holiday overtones has exactly the opposite effect on others.

The other example is a little known fall run of lunker brown trout up the Johns River, also a Lake Memphremagog tributary. The fish do not appear in large numbers, but they run up to a dozen pounds in weight. A fair number are taken each September by fishermen who know of the opportunity and who have the patience to endure many fishless hours for a single fish of great size.

Now, and much more to the point, let's examine those habits which all three species share in common, and the ways in which these habits can be exploited.

Elementary as it may seem, it is well to point out that stream trout invariably lie facing the current. Their concentration is focused upstream

Spring spawning urge in rainbows produces early fishing on Vermont's Willoughby River. Vermont Fish & Game Department.

Vermont fisheries biologist Angelo Incerpi weighs rainbow caught in early Willoughby River season.
Vermont Fish & Game Department.

as they continually inspect the descending flow for whatever food items it may bear. In general, therefore, the fisherman stands a somewhat lesser chance of spooking trout by his approach if he fishes upstream. This is by no means an absolute, mind you, but it is one of the little differences that add up to a big total in trout fishing.

Now, since we hope to catch trout by the mouth, what do they eat? Without stretching the truth too much, the answer could be: "Almost anything." I can say this with some authority, for while cleaning trout I can seldom resist the urge to slit their stomachs and examine the contents. The bulk, by far, is insect life—of various kinds and in one form or another —but I have found much else. Gut-clogging filter tips of cigarette butts, for one thing. Buttons, pieces of glass, chunks of bark, pebbles—only introductory to the total conglomeration I have observed.

Last opening day I caught a mess of brookies from a little stream which empties into a warm water pond. Sunfish had worked their way up the stream, and darned if the two largest brookies weren't stuffed with half-dollar size sunnies!

But although perhaps interesting, the eccentricities of trout appetites is not properly our concern here. The main dish, the meat and potatoes so to speak, is what we are out to identify. The answer, as already indicated, is a steady diet of insects.

Usually the contents of a trout's stomach is such a "mishmash" that individual items are almost indistinguishable. For much easier identification, drop the contents into a bottle of clear water and shake gently. What seemed to be little more than a blob of dark pulp will separate into the recognizable corpses of different kinds of insects in various stages of metamorphosis. Some will have been scrounged from the bottom, some intercepted on their way to the surface and some snatched from the surface while on the verge of flight.

This aquatic insect life, in its various kinds and stages, is the food upon which trout depend for sustenance, day in and day out, summer and winter. And this, for our purpose, can be regarded as a crack in their defense. We can, we like to think, lead them to their downfall by gearing our wiles to this inherent monotony of diet.

A few other points are to be taken into consideration, however. Just as our billfolds reveal the ones, fives and tens we have, rather than the bills of larger denomination we'd *like* to have, the contents of a trout's stomach indicates a choice of what was available, but not necessarily certain exotic items often favored above all others. The earthworm is a noteworthy example. It is never present in a stream save by accident, but it is snapped up eagerly by trout when it does appear. Small bait fish are another example. They are seldom abundant in trout streams, and in order to chase and catch them trout must risk exposure. Consequently, they do not show up in trout stomachs with any regularity, but a minnow, alive or dead, can be a fetching bait when manipulated to within easy reach of a hiding trout.

Finally, there is the matter of flash and glitter. It is a known fact that trout are often excited into striking so-called "hardware"—spoons, wobblers and spinners geared to the size of the quarry. This peculiarity is not deducible from stomach contents. Yet it must be taken into consideration for our purpose, which is to induce trout to strike our hooks by whatever means we can bring to bear.

By and large, however, a major portion of our angling efforts will be aimed at exploiting trout hunger, so perhaps we should investigate briefly the matter of appetite fluctuations. At what particular times, if any, are trout most likely to feed?

I think that most trout fishermen would agree that somewhere, in any given stream at any given time, some trout are eating something. Although this dodges the question momentarily, it is a truth from which an axiom of enormous value can be inferred: *Keep plugging!* The trout fisherman who gives up easily usually gets no more than he deserves—an empty creel. The fellow who keeps forever trying always stands a chance, no matter how poor the conditions or dim the prospects. Every now and then he will cash in handsomely, which, in all justice, is the way it should be.

Specifically, or perhaps "generally" is a better term, trout can be expected to feed heavily at the following times and under the following conditions: During the early afternoon in early season, when the sun has had time to take the chill of freezing nights from the water. Later in the season, trout tend to feed early in the morning and after sundown. During and after a heavy shower which roils the water, trout can be expected to feed avidly at the bottom. At times of heavy mayfly hatches they will stuff themselves at the surface.

Since trout are cold-blooded creatures, whose bodily temperatures rise and fall with that of the water which they inhabit, it is not surprising that water temperature is a major determinant of their appetites. Generally speaking, trout remain rather sluggish, and feed with comparative indifference, when the water temperature is less than 50 degrees. Temperatures of over 65 degrees have much the same effect on appetites plus the added effect of driving trout deep in search of spring holes and cooler water. The middle ground, from roughly 50 to 65 degrees, gives the trout fisherman his best chances, although there is a phenomenon associated with ideal temperatures of which the fisherman should be aware.

Trout appetites increase enormously while water temperature is rising from the too-cold level to the optimum level. Hatchery personnel take advantage of this peculiarity by greatly increasing rations during the temperature rise and thereby producing larger trout in a given time than would otherwise be possible. From the fisherman's standpoint, he can work this knowledge to advantage by fishing, if possible, when temperatures are rising toward optimal but have not yet leveled off. Oddly enough, trout appetites subside considerably when this last occurs, although they will continue to feed at a normal rate as long as the new temperatures neither fall nor become excessive.

Trout are unable to survive in what are usually thought of as *warm water fisheries*—lakes and streams where water temperatures soar into the 80's and there is no stratification to furnish the relief of cool depths, and where only bass, pike, perch and other warm water species can live. Consequently, as the surface layers of trout waters approach such temperatures, trout immediately seek relief in spring holes and strata of lower temperatures. They continue to feed, once they move to suitable temperatures, but the problem of locating them makes the warm weather trout fishing of lakes and ponds very difficult.

Trout streams must remain reasonably cool by definition, but they vary considerably in this respect. The hottest weather may virtually kill the fishing temporarily in some streams while others, whose waters remain appreciably cooler, may still furnish reasonably good fishing, even during hot spells.

By way of brief summary: Trout feed indifferently in temperatures below 50 degrees (early season). In such temperatures, fish slowly and as close to the bottom as possible. Give plenty of time to each location. Trout feed most avidly when the temperature is climbing into the 50's and it behooves the fisherman to ply his wares at such times whenever possible. Good fishing will persist as long as the water remains between the mid-fifties and mid-sixties. Higher temperatures drive trout into spring holes and the depths, with success becoming a matter of finding them.

The foregoing should not be taken as an attempt to discourage trout fishing save when water temperatures are optimum. We would do but little trout fishing if we always awaited ideal conditions. In fact, one of the biggest challenges of the game is that of producing results when conditions are against us. Again, always remember that in any trout stream worthy of the name, somewhere a trout is feeding. To the dedicated trout fisherman, trout fishing is a never-ending search for that particular trout, wherever and whenever the opportunity arises.

Even though we may now understand the broad effects of water temperature, we must regretfully accept the fact that its rise and fall is quite beyond our control. Now we shall take a look at another factor which enters into the business of trout fishing, one with which we must cope but whose negations we can partially nullify if we take certain precautions.

The eternal presence of trout in our waters is more than a tribute to hatcheries, for in many streams and lakes of the northern New England states there exist wild trout populations that are self-sustaining despite heavy fishing pressure. Far from catching every trout in each stream, fishermen are denied perpetually by many trout which die of old age, simply because they have been deterred from suicidal foolhardiness on every occasion by either fear, or, its close relative, suspicion. Were it not for this pair of incredibly alert sentinels, trout fishermen would have little difficulty catching every last trout in each of our trout waters.

Fear and suspicion! The techniques of trout fishing are never more than ruses designed to circumvent these twin guardians of trout safety. We shall deal with the basics of these techniques in the chapters which follow, but in preparation it is important at this point to appreciate the enormity and complexity of the obstacle which they, the techniques, have been designed to overcome.

In other words, do not make the nearly fatal mistake of assuming that because trout are simple creatures fooling them is a simple process. To the contrary, trout are hard to fool because they *are* simple.

One shrewd poker player can "con" another equally shrewd opponent by cleverly exploiting an intelligence that is open to subtle manipulation through suggestion. A master trapper can lure the sliest fox into a trap by playing on its curiosity. But trout, because they are essentially witless, are open to no such ploys.

Their chief defense is not intelligence, but rather an incredibly keen sense of discrimination which enables them to detect the slightest deviation from the norm within the context of their concern. Making it tough for fisherman is the fact that the trout react to all that is only slightly abnormal by usually either downright fright, or suspicion that thwarts the angler's intent just as effectively. Either response prompts them to leave strictly alone any item, no matter how tempting it may be otherwise, which behaves in only a somewhat unnatural manner.

We shall take a long, hard look at "drag" later on, but for purposes of illustration here let it be introduced merely as a deviation from a fly's natural drift caused by the contrary influence of the line and/or leader.

Trout are seldom moved to actual fear by a tiny dry fly which may "drag" only an inch or two from its expected path. But fully as disastrous from our point of view, they immediately become suspicious—and shun the fly as though they knew it were lethal.

That a determination of such firmness and finality can be made in the absence of conscious understanding is hard for us to accept. As humans, we are accustomed to reaching decisions, usually then only half-heartedly, after much conscious shuffling of indistinct pros and cons. Nevertheless, this unthinking discrimination between natural and unnatural is a trout's sole defense against the conniving fisherman's intellect. Puny though it may seem, after a half century of trout fishing, I can assure you that it is a beaut!

As a requisite for that which follows, therefore, I ask the reader's acceptance of the premise that the key to success in trout fishing is almost completely the matter of achieving a natural presentation of lure or bait. It is important for the beginner to accept this viewpoint at the start. Otherwise, he must waste much valuable time learning the hard way that the most tempting natural baits, and their most impeccable imitations, will all go begging whenever this vital requirement is violated or ignored.

I ask also, from the vantage point of experience, unlimited respect for the uncanny sensitivity of trout which allows them to deduce the aspect of artificiality from factors too subtle and slight to evoke human recognition. The reader may have to accept this on blind faith at the moment, but I can assure him that he will become convinced of its truth if he truly becomes a trout fisherman.

Finally, there is the matter of fluctuations in the feeding patterns of trout, and in those of other fish as well, which cannot be explained in terms of factors currently identifiable. That these periods do occur—interludes during which streams "come alive" with feeding fish—is a matter of common knowledge among fishermen of experience. Indeed, most fond memories of exceptional fishing have their origin in just such feeding sprees—and in the good fortune to be at the right place at the right time.

I have been chided for my romantic belief that these surges are induced by external influences which are as yet unknown. Nevertheless, I stand firm in my belief, and further, recommend its adoption, if only because, by virtue of mystery, it enhances the charm of fishing.

Regretfully, I cannot lend my support to the Solunar Theory of long standing, even though it is a step in the right direction. Its claim to validity has been refuted by its failure to win wholesale acceptance after many years during which significant reliability would have become overwhelmingly evident. Everybody "believes in" penicillin, for example, because its effectiveness is indisputably demonstrable. Fishermen will leap to accept the explanation of one of angling's great mysteries whose truth can be as clearly demonstrated.

But again, our proper concern is with more basic matters, so now let us move to the most elementary—one which should at least be understood if not actually mastered.

2

BAIT FISHING FOR TROUT

Hopefully, this chapter will be brief and to the point, its purpose neither a case for or against bait fishing. Rather, it will attempt to employ this phase of trout fishing as an area in which the basic problems of trout fishing can be examined with the least confusion and, therefore, can be best understood.

As an example, the possible causes for success or failure become confusingly divergent when the question centers around the use of a particular artificial fly. Did the trout refuse the fly because its pattern was momentarily unattractive, or its size and color offensive, or did he reject it because its less than perfect presentation aroused his suspicion? Or, did he *take* the fly because of its inherent physical appeal, or because the fisherman served it to him, the trout, in a flawless manner? The bilateral ramifications of the questions preclude satisfactory response.

No such duality confuses the issue when the offering is the real thing, some natural item of food highly favored by trout. Here desirability can be taken for granted; trout either accept or reject a natural offering solely on the quality of its presentation.

It is probably because of this genuine quality that bait fishing for trout is so often, but so erroneously, adjudged as the one phase of the sport of trout fishing which requires but little skill. Why does one need skill, the reasoning goes, to persuade a hungry trout to gobble what is obviously a live worm?

However, if my premise of the preceding chapter has been accepted, the answer is clear: *A natural presentation must be achieved, whether the lure is an imitation or a natural bait.*

Those fishermen who choose to begin as bait fishermen will soon discover the truth of the foregoing statement. There is always the fish to prove the exception, of course, but despite the natural appeal of genuine baits they will find that it is very difficult to fool a substantial number of trout in streams, ponds and lakes that are fished as hard as eastern waters are fished. Bait fishing can be very instructive, therefore, if an effort is made to account for failures which seem to be almost unaccountable. Why, for Pete's sake, was a juicy nightcrawler ignored in pool after pool of a stream famed for its trout population?

A few days ago I was working a dry fly on a nearby stream. I made a long cast to the head of a pool, trying to drop my fly as close to the overhung bank as possible. As often happens to me nowadays, I lost sight of the fly in the air. When I began stripping slack I suddenly realized that it had never reached the water at all; my leader angled upward toward a spot seemingly in mid-air. Closer investigation proved that the fly had snagged on a strand of monofilament which angled into the pool from an alder branch above. After hauling in the monofilament I found the hook end had been weighted by not one, but two, Dipsey sinkers, each heavy enough to plunge almost any bait to the bottom of a millrace. In all probability, difficulty in casting such a combination had resulted in the strange tangle.

In any event, here was evidence of some unknown fisherman who obviously believed that proffering a natural bait, probably a nightcrawler, was all that was required to take trout. I have no way of proving it, of course, but I would bet that he left the stream with a very light creel.

I would also bet that if the same fisherman sticks at the game he will eventually wise up to the fact that the trick of fishing bait close to the bottom (where, indeed, it should be fished), but in a manner which will win acceptance, is not to be solved by merely attaching one or more heavy blobs of lead to his line.

It is at this point that the beginning trout fisherman begins to understand what the game is all about. It is not enough to place a bait or lure before a hungry trout; any blockhead can do that. The trick is to disguise the artificiality of its presentation and to prevent, to the fullest extent possible, the behavioral anomalies which it tends to exhibit.

The farther one penetrates into the "sticks," the less bait fishermen tend to be looked down upon, and if the game of trout fishing is an honest game, that is the way it should be. In virtually all of the many small towns

18

of Maine, New Hampshire and Vermont there is almost certain to be one or more very skillful trout fishermen locally famed for their expertise. In the majority of instances these are likely to be bait fishermen. Most of us who have moved through bait fishing to a preference for fly fishing do not envy their successes, but we can respect their proficiency for its basis in skill, instead of in luck which is often supposed.

My home town of Pittsford, Vermont (you're in the "sticks" anywhere in Vermont by definition, for which praises be!) is no exception, boasting several bait fishermen of marked prowess. Our young Town Clerk is one, our not-so-young Road Commissioner is another and one of our oldest citizens is yet a third.

Unlike the erudite beginner, who jumps directly from the pages of angling rhetoric to the stream, these crafty fishermen do what they do, not because they have read that it should be done, but because they know exactly *why* they are doing it!

One of the three, for example, has adopted ultralight spinning tackle with especially deadly effect. Although I'm sure he is appreciative of the added thrills which result from the use of very light tackle, I'm equally positive that he made the switch for purely practical reasons.

Much experience had convinced him of the difficulty of fishing large, heavily weighted baits convincingly. Yet it was all but impossible to cast light, tiny baits on conventional spinning tackle. The fly rod offered a scarcely better alternative. Designed to drive out a fly, it is ill-suited for softly lobbing out baits that are small, delicate and hard to keep on a hook.

The ultralight outfit, with its "threadline" monofilament and soft, short rod, will flip a tiny bait to the head of a pool or run with a mere flick of the wrist. Once dropped, the bait tumbles toward the fisherman without drag while the small spinning reel handily takes in the slack.

Do not jump to the conclusion that the result is wholesale slaughter. Enough drag results, and enough artificiality is evident, to deter most of the trout in a given pool. But because the technique *approaches* perfection it steps up production significantly.

Instead of merely dunking worms and hoping for the best, these fishermen are forever experimenting with new baits and new methods of presentation. They know that a single salmon egg on a No. 14 hook can be as deadly as dynamite when handy currents are utilized to draw it close to the bottom without glaring influence of line and leader. A shucked-out caddis larva, although harder to fish, is even deadlier because of the trout's tendency to look with especially high favor on this particular tidbit. (Caddis larvae are the "stickworms" which are often seen clinging to the bottom in trout streams. They take their name from the woody cocoon in which they encase themselves and which closely resembles a short section of twig. Trout eat them, case and all, but not avidly. But when "shucked" the small, white larva is regarded as a delicacy.)

If what I have said about bait fishing for trout encourages the beginner to sample it as a step in his evolution as a trout fisherman, I suspect that I will have done him a service. To those of such intent I offer the following recommendations.

If possible, do your bait fishing in the small streams of Maine, New Hampshire or Vermont. These small streams, the last to still run cold and pure, are rapidly becoming the last stronghold of the native brook trout.

Here one need make no apologies for fishing with bait, for it is usually the only way one *can* fish. Bordering growth and overhang make all casting out of the question, and in places the tangle may be so thick that it is only with difficulty that a baited hook can be lowered into the water.

These are the places brookies love, however, and their coloration, deepened and intensified by the shade in which they dwell, gives each freshly caught fish the beauty of exquisite jewelry. Do not expect large fish; a ten-incher is a whopper. But they are every inch trout, from head to tail.

If anybody tries to tell you that worming a small, tangled stream for pan-size brookies is neither fun nor worthy of a grown man's serious attention, send him around to me. Such a cynic is a danger unto himself, and needs to be put straight.

Finally, fish for these small, wild trout with full assurance that they can teach you much about trout fishing. All the fundamentals are there, in every little mountain stream, for all who fish with perception and the desire to learn.

Much can be learned about trout from bait fishing.
Maine Department of Inland Fisheries and Game
Tom Carbone.

3

SPINNING FOR TROUT

It now seems incredible that I had neither seen, nor heard tell of, a spinning outfit until after the end of World War II. Nowadays almost every beginner does his first fishing with a spinning rod. The rig's popularity is easily understood for it makes casting absurdly easy.

When spinning tackle first became available New England trout began taking their lumps, believe you me! A hint of what lay in store for them already existed, for a few enterprising fishermen had experimented with tournament bait casting tackle and the light spoons and wobblers which this tackle enabled them to cast. Although the hardware employed had been designed for bass fishing, trophy trout pounced on it like tigers.

I remember fishing the Dog River, a stream which enters the Winooski River at Montpelier, Vermont. It was too early in the spring for productive fly fishing, and I returned to my car empty-handed as a pair of fishermen returned to theirs. Unlike me, they were heavily and gloriously laden!

They had been casting small brass spoons with tournament bait casting tackle, and they proceeded to show me three brown trout that rocked me back on my heels. I'm sure that not one of the trio of trout weighed less than 4 pounds! It is hard to reconcile my shocked surprise, but in those days the use of hardware for trout was virtually unthinkable, not because of any question of ethics, but because of the firm and general belief that trout never touched the stuff.

The incident took place just prior to our entry into World War II, and like many others in my age bracket, my fishing was rudely interrupted shortly thereafter. But I left for the Army with the picture of those browns carefully filed in my mind, and with the determination to get myself a piece of *that* particular action as soon as things returned to normal.

By the time the military turned me loose, however, the first spinning tackle was just becoming available. This simplified the project, of course, for instead of improvising with bass tackle I could start slinging hardware designed specifically for trout fishing. I couldn't wait to get started.

Never have fond dreams and hopes been more fully realized. Trout? *Man, I slaughtered 'em!*

I remember wading into the Lamoille River one June afternoon, in the vicinity of Johnson, Vermont. My first toss of a brass spoon produced a rainbow of over a pound. A few casts later the same spoon took a heavy jolt from a second rainbow, this one twice as large as the first. After moving downstream to the next pool I snagged a hog-fat brown which taped over twenty inches and which weighed 3½ pounds!

Other spin fishermen were experiencing the same wild results and talk soon sprang up about "banning those damned spinning rigs before every stream in the state is ruined!"

Again, however, it was the old story of underestimating the opposition. Trout have always managed to live in the presence of fishermen and they were not now about to succumb to gadgetry. Although spinning's surprise attack decimated their ranks temporarily, they were not long in regrouping and mending their defenses. In a surprisingly short time all that glittering hardware, which at first had been so fascinating and exciting, was being steadfastly ignored by all save an occasional lunkhead who couldn't seem to get the message.

This sudden transition is still an unsolved puzzle to those fishermen who lived through it. How could an edict commanding collective self-restraint have been imposed so swiftly and so successfully? It is one of the mysteries which makes trout fishing so fascinating. Furthermore, the edict remains in force to this day.

Just last evening I fished nearby Furnace Brook, an angler's counterpart of a busman's holiday, inasmuch as it followed a full day's stint at the typewriter struggling to put something of trout fishing into words. A fair hatch was on, and the browns and rainbows were coming to dry flies quite readily. I lost count, but I must have taken at least twenty nice trout in only a couple of hours.

My only competition came from a pair of spin fishermen who, try as they might, couldn't get so much as a rap from the many trout that were showing. They finally quit in disgust and began picking and eating the wild strawberries which grow along the stream's banks.

Such apparent apathy, or restraint, on the part of the trout, doesn't mean that eastern trout cannot be caught on spinning lures, but the originally overpowering appeal of spinning hardware has been long since whittled down to size. Mere casting and cranking back in is no longer enough to turn the trick; it usually takes trout fishing "savvy" and provocative touches to produce any substantial success.

It is important for the beginner to realize that in this department of the game he is not presenting a simulated item of food in the hope that it will be gulped unsuspectingly. The spinning lure's effectiveness lies in its ability to excite by erratic action, accompanied by a display of flash and glitter. No effort is made to achieve a "natural" behavior, for no trout will hit a spinning lure that is motionless or seriously lacking in action. On the contrary, departure from the ordinary is deliberately invoked to attract attention. The chief difficulty is that of staying on the proper side of the very thin line that separates action which excites from action which frightens.

Fishermen split down the middle when it comes to the matter of why fish, trout included, hit metal spoons and wobblers. Some insist that it is because they mistake these lures for baitfish. Others declare that it is ridiculous to believe that fish, with their uncanny powers of discrimination, would ever be guilty of so gross an error. Fish hit hardware, this group insists, because its strange action somehow excites them to a state of belligerence culminating in attack.

Which answer is correct is of no great import here. Suffice it to say that a tantalizing, erratic action wins the most strikes. Whether such action best imitates that of a baitfish or provokes strikes for some other reason is of no practical significance.

We will have our say about trout fishing tackle later on, so I shall merely mention here that my recommendation for spinning for trout would be an open-faced reel, a medium action, or light action, rod of 6½ feet and monofilament line of 6-pound test. Most spinning lures require snap swivels to prevent line twisting; select the smallest that will do the job so that the lure's built-in action will be hampered as little as possible.

The different kinds of spinning lures are almost beyond count, but for years my favorite lures for trout fishing have been, and still are, three lures of deadly, but simple, design put out by the Orvis Company of Manchester, Vermont: "Long Spoon," "Broad Spoon" and "Normal Spoon." They do not look particularly impressive, but if my experience is a valid criterion, they tend to draw well ahead of the competition over the long haul.

The spinning outfit is perfection itself as a casting tool, but to the

Long Spoon, Broad Spoon, and Normal Spoon lures.
The Orvis Company, Inc.

fisherman who grew up with fly rods and bait casting outfits, it is something of an abomination when it comes to handling hooked fish. The offensive difference is that with either fly rod or bait casting outfit a lifted finger or thumb instantly turns a rambunctious fish against a free running reel, while with spinning equipment one must depend on the mechanical innards of the reel, specifically the drag, to arbitrate the critical matter of give-and-take during a scrap with a good fish.

For this reason it is highly important to set the drag at the desired tension before beginning to fish; failure to do so can result in a brand of tragedy which I have seen enacted to the tune of heartbreak on more than one occasion. In my opinion it is much better to set the drag far short of the line's breaking strength than only a bit beneath it. When a good fish wallops a lure, considerable friction and inertia are added to the drag's tension, and if the original setting fails to allow for this difference the line is very likely to break.

One should lean toward drag softness even more with the use of lighter lines, for inertia and friction will remain constant and allowance must be made for this fact. It is much better that a hooked fish run wild during the first moments than to have him snap the line against poorly calculated resistance.

Finally, as in all fishing, check your knots for strength and holding power before making your first cast. Illustrations of the best fishing knots are available to fishermen on every hand, and it would be of no real service to reiterate them here. Time spent learning to tie these knots is well spent, indeed, but the fact remains that nylon monofilament should be looked on as treacherous stuff to tie. Even though directions may be followed to the letter, knots in nylon have a tendency to creep and slide. The fisherman has two options—retie any knot which fails to bite into itself and hold when subjected to a strong, steady pull, or discover the same knot's infidelity later when it suddenly lets go during a hectic scrap with a heavy fish. The first option is strongly recommended.

Until one gains some experience it is probably best to fish downstream, casting across the current and allowing the lure to sweep through a downstream arc. The deeper the lure runs the better, so reel very slowly while the lure cuts across the current. If the current is fairly strong the lure will run quite rapidly throughout its swing and few strikes may come during this interlude. However, if the lure's appearance arouses or excites a trout, the fish is likely to follow the lure over its arc. The critical moment comes when the spoon or wobbler has completed its arc and lies directly downstream. Now is the time to be a bit cagey.

If you reel too steadily and too rapidly, the alerted trout will detect no sign of weakness in the lure's strong and continued progress and is all too likely to lose interest. The extra touch here is to let the lure falter at the end of the swing. Quit reeling entirely and make the lure alternately dart ahead then fall back and downward by pumping or twitching the rod lightly against the direct pull of the current. The fluttering lure now appears to be exhausted, helpless, a circumstance to which nature responds not with mercy but with immediate attack. If you are in luck, your excited trout streaks in for the kill.

On the other hand, he may find the necessary courage yet lacking. With this in mind, make your upstream retrieve a slow affair, interspersed with frequent pauses to allow the lure to dance, fall back and even sink to the bottom. By fishing out retrieves carefully in this manner I have had many a hair-raising strike just off the tip of my rod from trout which most certainly trailed the lure throughout most of its entire course.

When you have developed a better "feel" for your tackle, upstream spinning can be undertaken—and should be. Action suffers, for the lure does not have the current to work against, but a definite gain results from the greater ease with which depth can be attained. By reeling only a bit faster than the speed of the current, and by pumping the rod steadily, it is possible to drift your fluttering and tumbling lure just above the bottom. This is an excellent way to lose lures to snags, of course, but it is an equally good way to provoke strikes from bottom-hugging trout if you can accept your losses with good grace.

While I have lost much of my original enthusiasm for spinning for trout, I do look upon my ultralight spinning rig as an important part of my trout fishing tackle. With the reel filled with 2-lb. test line, the tiny broomstraw of a rod will flip out lures which weigh as little as 1/32 oz.

The secret of the outfit's effectiveness lies in these tiny teasers, minature spoons, wobblers and spinners, none of which weigh more than ⅛ oz. For some reason, possibly an inherent reluctance to tackle trout with only a 2-lb. test line, ultralight spinning, despite its demonstrable effectiveness, has never gained widespread popularity. Consequently, trout see the little lures only infrequently and seemingly have not developed a mass aversion toward them as they have developed against spinning lures of conventional sizes. In fact, there are occasions when they seem to prefer them above all else.

A couple of years ago I was visiting my longtime friend, H. G. Tapply, at his home in Alton, New Hampshire. "Tap" and I share a love of canoes and the bog-prowling which they make possible, and on the afternoon I have in mind we were indulging this mutual whim. Our selected course was over a nearby stream which flowed slowly through a quaking swamp-land and which was blocked here and there by beaver dams, some old, some new.

Tap was paddling, while I, the privileged guest, fished from the bow. It was a rather cold day, and with no insects hatching we could expect but few trout to show at the surface. Consequently, I was making "blind," upstream casts with my ultralight spinning rig, but a fly rod, rigged with a dry fly, lay ready in the bottom of the canoe.

We went troutless for a rather discouraging distance when, suddenly, as we rounded a bend, we were greeted by a beautiful sight in the pool ahead: the oily, bulging rises of a bulky trout. I quickly switched to the fly rod, and seconds later a high-riding dry fly was floating pertly over the trout's nose.

It had seemed to be about as close to a sure thing as you can encounter in trout fishing, but for some reason known only to himself the feeding trout would have absolutely nothing to do with my fly, despite what seemed flawless service.

Finally, Tap could stand the impasse no longer. "Why don't you show him that spinning lure?" he said.

I showed the fly rod reluctantly and flipped the tiny lure toward the head of the pool. *Wham!* A brook trout some fourteen or fifteen inches long, with the deep body of a bass, smacked the little spinner before I had cranked the reel handle more than a couple of turns!

Early one spring I was a guest of Lynn and Nina Tanner at their fishing camp on Long Pond in Jackman, Maine. The Moose River flows through Long Pond, and our main objective was the salmon which inhabit the river in various hotspots.

However, Little Churchill Stream enters the pond close to the Tanners' camp, and it teems with brook trout which, if not large, still make interest-ing fishing. Unfortunately, it was too early and cold for fly fishing.

I inquired about the possibility of using spinning tackle, but I could see that Lynn didn't take to the suggestion. He feared that the treble hooks would kill every trout hooked, he told me.

When I showed him the tiny lures I would like to try, he quickly relented. The trout in that little stream all but fought over the little spin-ners, and I had a field day. And although Lynn watched critically while I unhooked and released the first few, his doubts seemed to vanish as he observed how little damage was done by the very small, light wire, treble hooks.

I still value the little outfit for the purposes implied by these two examples: as a probing and prospecting tool for days when no fish are showing, and as an alternative to bait fishing during the early part of the season when the water is too cold for fly fishing. In the last instance, oddly enough, the little spinners will arouse trout from their lethargy, and provoke zooming strikes near the surface when no amount of fly fishing can achieve the same results.

Among the thousands of lures that human ingenuity has produced, and among the thousands to follow, only a comparative handful seems destined to achieve lasting reputation. For each one which wins permanent space in most tackle boxes, thousands are tried and soon forgotten.

Among a lesser number of ultralight lures there is one that I do not hesitate to recommend above all others I have used: the "Panther Martin," distributed by Harrison-Hodge Industries, Inc., St. James, New York, and now being made available by a growing number of retail outlets.

Panther Martin lure.
Harrison-Hoge

For years, this tiny lure has been my ace-in-the-hole with respect to ultralight spinning. Its construction is unique: a spinner blade with a reverse bend which, instead of being attached by a clevis, is pierced, and thus held, by the shaft upon which it turns. Its turning sets up a turbulence which can be felt via the rod and which, apparently, accounts for its special appeal. It has been slow to gain the recognition it deserves, but recent advertising in national outdoor magazines has brought it to the attention of fishermen in general.

Two more comments about the ultralight phase of the game and we'll have done with spinning.

When snap swivels are used they should be very tiny to permit maximum lure action. Some lures—the Panther Martin is one—are best fished with no swivels at all.

Finally, do not be deterred by the fragility of the threadline outfit. In fly fishing, large trout are whipped down by leaders of 2-lb. test, so the compromise of a 2-lb. test line is by no means unique. If the drag is reliable, and has been set properly, you can outlast a very heavy fish in open water just by remaining cool and playing a careful game of give-and-take.

As always, however, staying cool is usually the hard part!

4

WET FLY FISHING, PHASE I

If the "Phase I" has you puzzled, here's the reason for it. I have tried to proceed in the order which seems most logical, and to continue in this manner it seems necessary to divide wet fly fishing for trout into two parts.

It is logical for the beginner to do his first fly fishing with wet flies, but this should not be taken to mean that wet fly fishing is relatively simple in its entirety. On the contrary, it becomes extremely subtle and difficult in its upper reaches, and I think that the progressing trout fisherman should have a good dose of *dry fly* fishing before trying to cope with wet fly fishing at its trickiest. So let's have at it.

We will deal with fly fishing tackle later on, so let's take a balanced outfit for granted. The trick now is to learn to cast.

Much has been written by way of instruction, all with the best of intentions but, I strongly suspect, of but negligible aid to those who most need it. The truth is that the task of casting a modest length of fly line is a simple thing to learn for those to whom it comes naturally and easily, while for those of less aptitude it ranges from difficult and frustrating to downright impossible.

To those who can capture the timing (the key to the whole process), tossing out 30 to 35 feet of line, all that's needed in most situations, seems virtually effortless, as indeed it is—just a puff of effort while the rod does the work. Yet I've known strong men who could never master the knack and who couldn't cast a fly 40 feet if their lives depended on it. I even know of, through hearsay, a well-known fishing author and authority whose

Only slight effort drives line forward. Looks easy, but some find it difficult.
The Orvis Company, Inc.

Backcast provides leverage.
The Orvis Company, Inc.

unimaginable awkwardness with a fly rod comes as a painful shock to all who first behold it.

The theory is simple and easily stated. Toss the line behind you with a quick lift of the rod; pause for the backcast to extend; come forward against the inertia of the extended line. If all goes well, the line will flip forward and straighten at the expense of about as much exertion as is required to strike a match.

The only way to find out if it is going to work that way for you is to try it and see, preferably in private. If all the steps seem sensible, natural and therefore easy, and if you're laying out a modest length of line after a little practice, then you have it made. But if you're working like hell, whooshing the rod back and forth mightily, and the line refuses to *go* anywhere, then you're in trouble and I shall not attempt to assure you otherwise.

I can only tell you this: *The answer does not lie in working harder!* If you can't lay out 20 or 30 feet of line with only the tiniest bit of effort, you aren't going to *muscle* it out and there's no sense trying. Keep your effort slight while you feel for the right timing that will make all fall into place. Unlike some advisors, however, I'm not going to tell you that it's easy if you have no physical empathy for the job; I can only wish you luck and the courage to keep trying.

Fly fishing for trout can be divided into two general categories: that which is imitative in intent and that which is not. The latter demands substantially less skill and savvy, and it is to this division that this chapter will be devoted.

The term "wet fly" is a loose one if it is taken to mean all kinds of flies (another loose term) designed to be fished under the water rather than to float at the surface. If we apply this definition, our list of wet flies must include not only the standard patterns (Montreal, Royal Coachman, Silver Doctor and the like) but also bucktails, streamers, nymphs and any other furred and feathered lures designed for underwater use.

For the sake of simplicity we will narrow the definition for the moment to include only the standard wet fly of traditional design: tail, body, flat, turned-down wings, and a hackle that is drawn downward and backward to form a tuft under the foremost part of the wings.

The reason for this particular design has long been lost and forgotten, but it has been followed faithfully for centuries. Oddly enough, the design is not even roughly imitative of any known form of trout food. Even stranger, perhaps, is the fact that many generations of anglers have fished these flies with unswerving faith in their imitative qualities without the slightest notion of what they, the flies, actually imitate!

Back in the days when standard wet flies were the fly fisherman's only ammunition, a solemn liturgy evolved pertaining to their use which added to the romance of fly fishing if not to the science of the sport. The names of popular patterns became hallowed symbols—Parmachene Belle, Silver Doctor, Professor, Montreal, McGinty—and a blind faith in their omnipotence was expected. Many a heavy creel was smugly attributed to the right choice, at the right time, from among a long list of gaudy, nonimitative patterns.

Standard wet fly. Non-imitative design of ancient origin is still held sacred.
The Orvis Company, Inc.

Perhaps the oddest thing is that these flies were successful, even though they were fished in a most unlikely manner. This consisted of darting and skittering them along the surface, an action effected by none of the insects upon which trout feed. The fact remains, however, that standard wet flies fished in this way took trout. Furthermore, they still will.

Few experienced fly fishermen fish wet flies in this way today, but it makes an excellent starting method and place for the beginner. Also, it is a mighty exciting way to take trout.

I remember some moments of just such exciting fishing while on a canoe trip on the Moose River near Jackman, Maine. We made side trips to outlying small ponds, and on one of these we were having no luck until I spotted a small inlet, the mouth of which was all but overhung by the thick puckerbrush. Our guide slid the canoe within casting range and I dropped my wet fly in the very narrow channel. At the very first "skitter" a foot-long brookie charged with a shower of spray and a great show of orange belly. More casts proved the inlet to be full of trout, and because of my vantage point in the bow I was "forced" to do all the fishing. When they finally stopped hitting we had all the red-fleshed trout that three of us could eat that evening at supper.

Incidentally, it is worth a moment's digression to note that wilderness ponds, even though they may teem with brook trout, can be mighty tough to cope with at times. Although the brook trout is sometimes rated as a comparatively easy mark, those which inhabit ponds such as we are discussing can be about as difficult to take as any trout I have come up against.

At any rate, when such ponds seem barren of trout, salvation often lies around the mouth of any tiny inlet such as I have mentioned. These inlets are hard to spot in the thick brush which usually borders northern trout ponds, but the wise fisherman keeps his eyes peeled for them. Their discovery often means a day-saving interlude of the hottest kind of action.

Now, getting back to the use of the wet fly, my final reason for recommending it as a starting place is that I caught my first trout on a fly by twitching a Silver Doctor along the surface and know from experience the excitement of such a triumph. That first strike, a magnificent swirl, was to me a wonder to behold, and although my prize was only a 10-inch brookie, no trout since has handed me a greater thrill.

In preparation, I recommend the purchase of wet flies (unsnelled) in size 12. Pick your own patterns; it's fun, and you can't go wrong. Buy one or more 7½-ft. leaders, tapered to 2X. Tie your flies to the leader with a Turle knot. Remember to test for knot reliability.

Perhaps it should be noted that a leader tippet of 2X is fairly heavy and would be a poor choice if you were out to achieve a dragless presentation. Since you are not, the relatively great diameter will not count against you. Moreover, it will provide a cushion of added strength while your reflexes are conditioning to the restraint which must be used when setting the hook with leaders of lesser test.

For best results the stream of your choice should be no larger than necessary to provide ample casting room. Almost everything you will learn about trout fishing will be associated with certain water characteristics. This interdependence carries through an ever-shifting complex of depths, currents and cover, and these differences which make all the difference are most obvious and thus most easily learned in streams of relatively small flow.

Our chosen technique requires downstream fishing. You will therefore approach each pool from above. (Not good, from the standpoint of maximum stealth, but a necessary compromise in this case.) No two pools are exactly alike, of course, but in most the current funnels through a narrowed entrance, picking up speed as it goes, then spreads and slackens as the pool broadens and deepens. All items of trout food that are carried by the current must pour through the narrowed entrance, so it is only natural that hungry trout will be attracted to this run-in and its concentrated food content.

One may assume, and correctly, that such food-minded trout will station themselves just downstream from where the current sweeps into the pool, but this is not the whole truth. Other trout are very likely to position themselves immediately *above* the run-in. Here the water is usually shallow as it quickens before dropping into the pool, and food items are easily discerned by the waiting fish in this thin layer of fast moving water.

From as far upstream as you can manage comfortably, drop your first cast in this spot, which in Maine is called the "top of the pitch." Tighten your line, but instead of retrieving at once, keep the fly dancing and skittering at the surface by twitching your rod tip. If you get a strike, be advised that it will come with the unexpected suddenness of a thunderclap. Against the taut line and leader, the trout will either hook itself, or fail to do so, long before you can react. If the hook jabs home, and your rod plunges, you will know instantly why most trout fishermen eventually prefer fly fishing.

Continue downstream. Fish slowly and thoroughly. Cover the fast water at the head of the pool, the slower and broader body and finally the tail. Don't attempt to "read" the water at this stage of the game lest you jump to wrong conclusions. Instead, cover *all* of it methodically, and take careful note of the types of "lies" which tend to produce strikes and those which don't. Where currents are fast, retrieve very slowly; keep the fly dancing but let it gain a little, only to fall back, as though its upstream progress were achieved only by dint of hard struggle. Over relatively flat and calm water, retrieve at a considerably faster pace. Cast as much line as you can handle easily, but do not try to overreach.

Confine your next several forays *to the same stretch of the same stream.* Fish for trout, but fish harder to learn about trout fishing. Generalities will begin to take shape as you observe similar things happening in similar places. By using the same stretch of stream as your proving ground you will be able to distinguish that which happens rarely by coincidence from that which happens regularly, the true effects of recognizable causes.

I am fortunate enough to live almost within sight and sound of Furnace Brook, one of the most productive small trout streams in Vermont. For years I have fished the same half-mile stretch whenever the mood strikes me, which in late May and June is quite likely to be evening after evening. I never tire of it, for although by now I should know its every secret, it almost invariably springs one or more surprises on me each time I fish it.

Speed up learning by sticking to same small stream.
Bernard "Lefty" Kreh

If this is true of so short a stretch of small stream, one which I have fished hundreds of times, it is almost discouraging to reflect upon my ignorance and disadvantage on those larger and more distant streams which I fish with much less frequency!

Stick at your simple (?) wet fly fishing until you get the feel of your tackle and until you begin to feel a measure of empathy toward the trout and their nature. The latter will include a growing awareness of the locations in a stream which they prefer for feeding stations, a beginning understanding of why they choose such spots and the increasing ability to distinguish and recognize these places as you come to them. You will also develop the ability to estimate how close you can approach such spots without spooking the trout they hold, and how much, or how little, sloppiness in your overall performance will be tolerated.

You may even build up preferences among fly patterns, most of which will be bunk. Small matter! All of us do it, to one degree or another, and it adds to the intrigue of the game.

Finally, before you fish long, you will observe steadily rising fish which will have absolutely nothing to do with your wet fly, even though you twitch it over and among them repeatedly. You will then realize that the kind of wet fly fishing you are doing, while it may have its good points, becomes ineffectual at trout fishing's most interesting and challenging point: when trout are feeding at the top, boiling the surface with their rises as they suck in mayflies. Suddenly you are caught up by the urge to deal with those feeding trout on their own terms, and now it is you, the fisherman, who is hooked for life. We shall take up the next step in your evolution presently.

But before taking leave of this first phase of fly fishing, it will be well to experiment a bit with another of its variations, the use of bucktails and streamers.

The streamer, and its deerhair relative, the bucktail, deserve special mention in any book of eastern trout fishing. The streamer is a New England creation, conceived for the taking of landlocked salmon and lake trout near the surface during the early spring. The original idea was to imitate smelt, the fish upon which the landlocked salmon and lakers of northern lakes depend for sustenance. The innovation was an immediate success. Fly rod trolling with streamers and bucktails is now the standard method of fishing for landlocks for as long as they remain near the surface.

In days gone by, practically all Maine salmon lakes also held a substantial population of large brook trout, and it was quickly observed that the streamers were as effective among the trout as among the salmon. This led to the trial of smaller sizes on streams and trout ponds, and it soon became

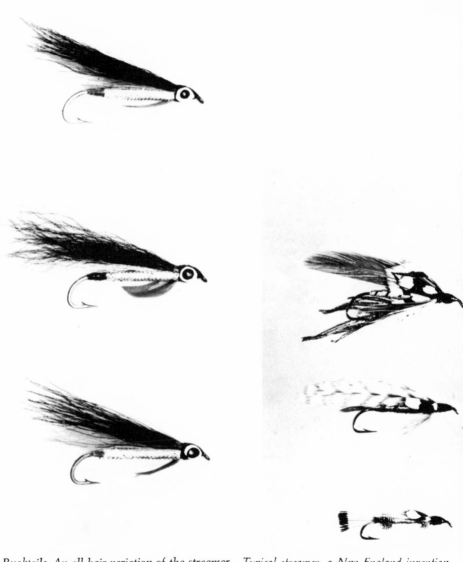

Bucktails. An all hair variation of the streamer.
The Orvis Company, Inc.

Typical streamer, a New England invention.
The Orvis Company, Inc.

apparent that streamers and bucktails were effective trout-takers when due allowance in fly size was made for the size of the trout being fished for.

Whether a streamer or bucktail is actually mistaken for a smelt or other baitfish is a question too controversial to debate here, for it is impossible to settle it to everybody's satisfaction and would serve no real purpose were it possible to do so. The important thing is that if you work a streamer or bucktail with a darting action which allegedly imitates that of a minnow, trout will smack it with some regularity.

If you suspect that your selected testing ground holds some lunkers, give a No. 6 streamer a try, or come on even stronger with a No. 4. Streamer patterns are many and faniciful, but like standard wet flies, of one general design. Whether one pattern is better than another is always highly questionable. All will take fish, so make your choice with that assurance. Fish the streamer exactly as you have fished your wet flies. If something huge rises up and clobbers it you're in for a major thrill.

Trophy trout are rare items nowadays, so don't be disappointed if you draw a blank. But before quitting with streamers, give those of smaller size a try. Where trout of the usual run predominate, eight to twelve inches, either a No. 8 or a No. 10 is appropriate. Judging from my experience, the small streamers will take somewhat fewer fish than did the wet flies, but the average size will be a notch or two larger.

Maybe what I have to say now should have been said at the beginning of this chapter in order to set the reader's mind at rest concerning any special skills that are needed to play and land fish on a fly rod.

Be assured that the fly rod's apparent fragility is deceptive. Instead of compromising the fisherman, it actually gives him a tremendous advantage in handling hooked fish. The fly rod's pliancy makes it possible to maintain a constant pressure against the fish, yet one which is fully cushioned against sudden dashes and unexpected shows of strength. With a reel filled with fly line and backing, it is only necessary to allow fish to run against the click and drag of the reel whenever the strain on the rod becomes dangerous. Each run takes its toll from the fish's reservoir of energy, and eventually it will become utterly exhausted and can be netted.

Remember that Atlantic salmon weighing 20 pounds and more are caught regularly on ordinary fly rods. It would be disastrous to snub these tremendously fast and powerful fish on *any* tackle, but they can't break even the lightest fly rod if they are never given direct leverage against it. Instead, they eventually tire themselves by their wild leaps and sizzling runs which, if the reel is managed properly, do not endanger the rod.

Of course, if you choose to make an engagement with a large fish a test of strength, the fly rod is no tool for the job. Every guide has a sad tale about some poor soul or other who lost the prize of a lifetime by refusing to yield so much as an inch of line from a well-filled reel.

Again, the secret is to stay cool—which is sometimes the hardest trick in the book!

Pliancy of sensitive fly rod is actually an advantage in playing fish.
The Orvis Company, Inc.

5

DRY FLY FISHING

Most fly fishermen would rather take trout on dry flies than by any other method. Some, myself included, become so partial to the use of dry flies that they act to their own disadvantage by stubbornly trying to take trout on dries when wet flies, nymphs or streamers would bring better results.

Probably the biggest reason for this preference is the high degree to which the most exciting action in dry fly fishing is *visible.* Usually, or at least frequently, the dry fly fisherman brings his talents to bear on a fish of known position, and sometimes of predetermined size. Such fish can be spotted in advance, rising to mayflies in positions which lie upstream from the angler. The interlude during which the latter moves carefully to within casting range is one of exotic anticipation, particularly if the trout goes on rising steadily and its rises are deliberate and "bulgy," clearly indicating a fish of considerable bulk.

If all goes well, the fly drops lightly above the trout and visibility continues to be a titillating factor as the fly's smooth drift toward the trout is watched with mounting suspense and excitement.

Finally, what is perhaps the greatest moment of triumph in all trout fishing occurs when the deluded trout is *seen* to rise up and gulp the fly!

There is much more, of course: the feeling of elation as the rod bends against strong resistance; the trout's frantic bid for freedom, perhaps accompanied by wild leaps; the final moment of triumph as the exhausted trout is scooped up in the net. But all that which ensues *after* the moment of hooking is common to all fly fishing. Only in dry fly fishing is the "take" and its prelude fully as exciting as that which follows.

The reader may have been led to believe that dry fly fishing is significantly more difficult than other kinds of fly fishing, but this is largely false. True, the beginner's first efforts will leave much room for improvement. But if he has followed the recommendations of the preceding chapter, and has become moderately competent at casting, there is no reason in the world why he cannot now turn to dry fly fishing *and take trout from the outset.*

For as long as man has regarded trout with interest, which is to say for a very long time, indeed, he has observed them feeding on mayflies whenever hatches occur. Mayflies, of which there are many species, spend the major portion of their lives under rocks, or burrowed in the silt and gravel, at the bottoms of streams and lakes. They are called nymphs during this stage, and bear but small resemblance, if any, to the adult forms they will eventually attain.

This transition to adulthood involves a rise to the surface and perilous moments of drift while the nymph case splits and the winged adult, or *dun,* emerges. More dangerous moments pass while the vulnerable dun orients itself. Then, if it has been lucky enough to escape the eyes and maws of hungry trout, it becomes airborne and rises slowly from the water. Its safety is not yet assured, however, for it is all too likely to fall victim to the cruising swallows and other fly-catchers which are quick to patrol the air above a stream whenever a hatch is in progress.

If it does escape, the dun alights in a tree or bush near the stream where it molts a second time and attains its final adult form. In a day or two the survivors of the hatch return to the stream to perform a mating "dance," to deposit the eggs which will start another life cycle and then to die. During this final stage they are called *spinners.* Trout feed on them only listlessly, if at all. Their interest is chiefly in the duns which are apparently more appetizing and probably more nourishing.

Stated as simply as possible, dry fly fishing consists of employing floating imitations of the duns which the trout so relish, and of attempting to bamboozle the trout into gulping the imitations while under the impression that they are actual mayflies.

While fly fishing for trout has been going on for many centuries, dry fly fishing, as it is currently practiced, is a comparatively recent innovation. You can be certain that many past generations of trout fishermen, witnessing the inevitable rises to mayfly hatches, longed for the *means* of dry fly fishing, but in vain. Only in this century has our technology reached the point where the necessary materials of dry fly fishing have become sufficiently available to permit wholesale adoption of the technique.

It would be hard for many living today to picture a world without nylon, but this material became generally available hardly more than three decades ago. In the pre-nylon days, leaders were made from silkworm gut, a material which usually was of uncertain thickness unless diamond drawn, and which had to be well soaked prior to use. Fly lines were also of silk, with finishes greatly inferior to those of today. Silk lines were hard to float, and they deteriorated with age.

Move backward in time as many years again and leaders, lines, rods and even most available reels, were almost hopelessly unsuitable for dry fly fishing.

Excellent tackle and equipment poses no problem nowadays. Good rods, reels, lines, leaders and flies are available in abundance at reasonable prices. I might add that they are also available at outrageously high prices, but there is no need for the dry fly fisherman of limited means to indulge in extravagant tackle.

As we prepare to look into dry fly fishing it is important to recognize this distinction: Our strategy now becomes imitative in nature. We will no longer be relying on lure action to rouse trout to the point of attack. On the contrary, we will attempt to persuade trout that our imitations are the real thing, and we will count our triumphs as complete only when our flies are taken calmly and deliberately, by fish which are confident that they are genuine mayflies.

In your introductory wet fly fishing you were permitted considerable latitude of execution. If, in one way or another, you gave your fly an erratic action a trout was likely to grab it. In dry fly fishing, it is so seldom that trout will rise to a "skittered" dry fly that most dry fly fishermen resort to a jerky retrieve only as a final, and usually futile, ploy when all real hope has faded. Instead, they try to avoid all "action" completely, especially the dragging effect of leader and line which is the usual cause for rejection.

This odd difference is difficult, if not impossible, to explain, and remains one of the many mysteries of trout fishing. Perhaps it is because trout which are feeding on mayflies have, of necessity, positioned themselves somewhat dangerously and are especially cautious and discriminatory. They may thus honor their vulnerability by instinctively rejecting anything and everything save the mayflies which they *know* to be innocuous. This guess is perhaps supported by the fact that trout would grab your skittered wet fly when not preoccupied with a hatch, but would steadfastly scorn it while feeding on mayflies.

In making the transition from wet fly fishing to dry fly fishing it is important to accept the fact that you are moving to a context of much stricter discipline and greater circumspection. Even with this accepted, at the outset you are almost certain to underestimate the narrowness of definition which surface feeding trout place upon acceptability. Should this be the case, you are likely to meet with wholesale refusal until you finally toe the mark and shape your presentation so as to come within the limits of this definition. There is no other road to success; sheer persistence will get you nowhere for as long as it incorporates sloppiness.

In the first chapter a brief reference was made to "drag" as a departure from the normal float or drift of the fly which is caused by the influence of line and/or leader. The time has come to take a long, hard look at what is probably the most important single factor in dry fly fishing.

A stream is always a veritable network of tiny, individual currents. Drop two bits of twig to the surface. They draw apart, speed up, slow down and even halt momentarily, not in unison, but according to respective patterns which differ significantly. Trout are incredibly sensitive to these separate currents, and to win their confidence and acceptance a dry fly must follow to the letter all of the shifting impulses of the current on which it drops. It need only move an inch or two "thisaway," when the current is moving "thataway," to put trout on guard, if not down.

To illustrate, let's assume an exaggeration. Contrary to normal procedure, you approach a rising trout from *upstream*. You cast downstream to the fish and your dry fly drops lightly and accurately. But then line and leader come taut. Instead of drifting downstream, the fly hangs in one spot (over the trout) while the current slides under it. The imitative appearance of the fly has not been changed by the check of line and leader; it looks as much like a mayfly as it does while floating freely. Yet trout, except in the rarest of instances, will have nothing to do with it. They are not deterred because they deduce the fly's deadly implications; they reject it purely on the grounds of suspicion, aroused by its unnatural behavior alone.

Therefore, no dry fly fisherman compromises his chances by fishing downstream. However, trout often take up feeding positions which make a dragless float very difficult for the angler who is fishing upstream.

In "my" stretch of Furnace Brook there is a fine pool, at the head of which the current collides solidly with a jutting ledge. The main flow sweeps around the point, but another part is shunted to one side where it forms a backwater whose direction of flow is precisely opposite that of the main stream.

Trout love to lie in this backwater and pick up the food items which are circulated therein. The approaching fisherman is often treated to the sight of their rises, but unfortunately his only feasible approach is along the opposite side of the stream. It is always tempting to cast across the main current to trout rising in the backwater, but it is almost invariably futile.

In this situation, as in its many counterparts which exist in all trout streams, the main body of the line falls across the downstream current while the fly drops on water moving in the opposite direction. The line is quickly carried downstream, of course, and this drags the fly against the direction of the backwater. Once in a great while a trout will make a dive for the fly, almost always missing it. But for the most part, it is merely an exercise in futility.

Once, last season, the rise of what looked like a particularly good trout prompted me to act more intelligently. I crossed the stream well above the pool, and returned. I was now *facing* the flow of the backwater and my fly floated nicely. The fish, which took on the first pass of the fly, proved to be a rainbow of about 14 inches.

One of the first requirements of successful dry fly fishing, therefore, is that of picking the casting position which seems to promise minimum interference from troublesome cross currents. A further point: When you have selected what *appears* to be the best vantage point, do not hold to that opinion in the face of repeated refusals. Drag too slight for you to detect may be gumming up the works. Shift your position a bit. Quite often this will eliminate the source of drag and result in a prompt rise.

Sometimes, however, acceptance follows refusal for reasons much harder to account for.

I recall fishing a pool last June where a dandy trout was gulping may-flies as fast as he could tip up for them. I put cast after cast over his busy nose, but although I could detect no flaw in the drifting fly he scorned it repeatedly. I shifted my position slightly, but to no avail. In the meantime, he calmly went on rising, sometimes taking a natural only inches from my floating fly.

Although I knew that far more cooperative trout awaited in upstream pools, I couldn't bring myself to walk away from so fine a fish while it was rising steadily. Finally, after goodness knows how many fruitless casts, the trout, a handsome sixteen-inch brown, nonchalantly sucked in the very fly which he had for so long, and so repeatedly, rejected. Why?

The question is unanswerable, but in the enigmatic outcome of the incident lies a truth of great importance to the dry fly fisherman: For as long as your casting does not put down a feeding trout, *each successive cast begins a brand new ball game.*

In other words, if my observations are valid, a feeding trout does not look upon a repeatedly presented fly as something which he has seen before and about which he has formed an opinion. Instead, he evaluates each drift of the same fly on its own merits alone, and is not in the least influenced by its past behavior. He will continue to reject it only as long as he detects in it grounds for suspicion. If, on perhaps the twentieth cast, he sees nothing wrong in its presentation, he is likely to gulp it without the slightest qualm.

Here, as at many other points in any discussion of trout fishing, much delightful speculation could ensue which would lead to no conclusion. For our purpose, and without trying to resolve the question, it behooves us to accept the lesson which is clearly implied: *Always fish carefully and thoroughly; carefully,* because a feeding trout is always a prospect until you alarm him and *thoroughly* because if you finally achieve near-perfection on your twentieth cast, the minor flaws of the preceding nineteen will not count against you.

We have defined dry fly fishing as imitative, but so far we have concerned ourselves only with "imitating" a natural drift of the fly. What about the fly's appearance, the degree to which it resembles an actual mayfly?

Here we come to a matter which the fisherman can make as complex as he chooses. In the first place, there are many species of mayflies. All differ in one or more respects, and the dry fly fisherman can become very deeply involved in attempting to identify them if he so desires. Then, identification achieved, he can become further entangled in the complex and demanding task of trying to do justice to these small differences in his imitations. On the other hand, relatively few species of mayflies make up the bulk of a trout's diet and these few have much in common. The fisherman who likes to keep things simple can do so by concentrating on these few important species and on imitating only their general characteristics.

Since many dry fly fishermen and fly-tiers gain maximum pleasure by adopting the first named point of view, it goes almost without saying that hundreds of dry fly patterns exist. Unlike the hundreds of patterns of wet flies, each dry fly pattern, save for a few exceptions (Royal Coachman is one example), is imitative by design and bespeaks conviction of the need for an imitation of each mayfly species.

This brings us to the matter of "matching the hatch," the subject of endless debate among dry fly fishermen. Some fishermen place the utmost importance on accurately matching whatever species of mayflies is emerging and a lifelong search for the most effective imitations is incorporated in their efforts. Others content themselves with a few basic patterns and pin their faith on fishing these as flawlessly as possible.

Dry fly imitates the live insect only by approximation. Exact imitation is neither possible nor necessary.
The Orvis Company, Inc.

Regardless of the respective merits of these opposing schools of thought, the beginner's salvation lies in the fact that a few basic patterns will meet his immediate needs.

Most of the early hatches are made up of mayflies which are dark in color, colors that range from nearly black, through slate grey, to what can be called rusty brown. Adequate imitations can be selected from the following short list of patterns: Black Gnat, Quill Gordon, March Brown, Hendrickson (dark), Nearenuf and Adams. Later in the season, lighter flies appear—and late evening fishing becomes the best bet. Here the Light Cahill not only fills the imitative need but is more easily followed than darker patterns in the dim light.

If I seem to oversimplify it is because I stand guilty as charged. There are unquestionably times when one *must* match the hatch accurately or go fishless, just as there are equally rare times when trout seem ready to take almost anything. A fisherman must experience both these extremes, and cover the middle ground which lies between, before deciding just what his attitude toward matching the hatch shall be.

In the meantime, however, the beginner's mind should not be cluttered by controversy. The short list of patterns, and the simple rules governing choice from among them, will suffice until personal convictions are shaped by experience.

Although you can always stir up a heated argument about the importance of pattern and pattern choice, virtually all dry fly fishermen are agreed upon the importance of size. Early season hatches are almost always made up of quite large mayflies. During this period, flies tied on No. 12 and No. 14 hooks will approximate the size of most of the hatching insects and will be taken readily.

The later hatches run to smaller mayflies, and usually you must match the hatch in size, even though you may not have to do so in pattern. Why this is so has long defied explanation.

Large trout will sometimes feed on tiny flies when no larger flies are available, and this is understandable. But if in the midst of the unsubstantial midges there suddenly appeared a king-sized offering, it seems logical to assume that it would be snapped up eagerly. Oddly enough, the effect is invariably the opposite. The large fly, even though it floats perfectly, is shunned as completely as it would be if dragging badly.

On the Battenkill, for instance, trout can be seen dimpling the surface almost every evening, even into the hottest months of the summer. In many of its finest stretches its flow is almost a steady, unbroken march. Its surface presents few conflicting currents, and nearly dragless floats are the rule rather than the exception. On the other side of the coin, the clear water and the relatively unbroken surface give the trout the opportunity to give each passing fly a long, hard look—which is exactly what the cautious devils do.

On a late summer evening, when only tiny mayflies are hatching, you can all but wear out your arm without raising a fish if you use anything larger than a No. 18. Even while using 18s and 20s you will do no land-office business unless you are a better trout fisherman than most. But with the tiny flies you can take a few trout, whereas those large enough to seem tempting by human standards will be ignored completely.

We have defined drag as the influence which the leader tends to impart to the fly. It can be seen that the more flexible the leader, the freer the fly will be to respond to the whims of the current. The ideal safeguard against drag, therefore, would be a leader that was of very fine diameter throughout its entire length. Unfortunately, a leader of this construction would be impossible to cast properly; instead of straightening, "turning over," it would fall in a snarled heap at the completion of each cast.

To effect a workable compromise, leaders are designed so as to incorporate sufficient stiffness for "turnover" in the butt section and fine diameters in the forward part or tip to provide flexibility and delicacy of presentation. The result is a "tapered" leader, either a manufactured one of continuous taper or one tied from strands of nylon of progressively smaller diameters.

Most fishermen tie their own tapered leaders, tying a perfection loop at the butt, and securing the individual strands with a barrel knot. Unfortunately, a great many, myself included, are too sloppy to go about it scientifically. Instead of evolving a formula for best performance, we go at it "by guess and by gorry" each time. The result, of course, is a succession of leaders which work with varying degrees of efficiency when all should be uniformly satisfactory.

The trick, of course, is to produce a descending order of diameter in which each strand or section is capable of transmitting the energy of the cast to the next. Should one step-down be too abrupt, it will act as a hinge and allow the leader to fold back upon itself at that point.

Although I certainly knew better, I went on tying my leaders more or less haphazardly, with predictable results, until I ran across a strand-by-strand formula recommended by angling experts. This was in an issue of "The Fly Fishing Bulletin," circulated periodically by Scientific Anglers, Inc. of Midland, Michigan. With their permission, their recommended formula for a 9-ft. tapered leader to be used with a 6-weight line, shown on the next page, totals 7½ feet. The remaining 18 inches is made up by a tippet of that length which can vary from 3X to as fine as 7X. The 3X tests a fairly rugged 4 lbs. but the 7X tests only 1½ lbs. and is used only when very tiny flies make it a necessity. Neither 6X nor 7X tippets should be tied directly to the .010" tip of the basic leader as the large difference in diameter makes a trustworthy joining impossible. Instead, tie in 6" of 3X and then a foot of the whispy stuff.

Diameter of Material (inches)	Length of Strand (inches)
+ .021	18
+ .019	18
+ .018	18
+ .016	18
+ .014	7
+ .012	6
+ .010	5
	90

A long leader is of no advantage if it doesn't straighten. If you have trouble with the 9-ft. leader, I suggest shortening each of the four heavier strands by about four inches. The shorter leader will be adequate for most dry fly fishing. It will even be an advantage on small streams where a long leader becomes a nuisance whenever short casts are called for.

The manufacturers of spinning lines strive for limpness, whereas the nylon monofilament used for leader tying should exhibit a certain amount of stiffness in all but the tippet strands where flexibility is important. The bargain counter nylon, which is suitable enough for spinning, as well as the various weights of more expensive monofilament spinning lines, do not make up into good dry fly leaders. It is much better to obtain a kit consisting of spools of nylon made especially for leaders and ranging through all the necessary diameters. Incidentally, if you cannot find the exact diameters called for in the foregoing formula, substitutions of .001 inch, larger or smaller, can be made without affecting performance.

I tie my leaders made from such a kit which I obtained from the Orvis Company, Manchester, Vermont. Two other firms which offer leader material kits are Bruce B. Mises, Inc., 112 S. Robertson Blvd., Los Angeles, Calif., and Mason Tackle Co., Otisville, Michigan.

Since dry fly fishing is surface fishing, it is imperative that both line and fly float. (It is desirable that the leader should *sink,* but it often refuses to. My personal answer to this problem is to forget about it!) Fly line manufacturers supply preparations which help their lines to float and these should be applied before starting to fish. Dry flies will float by virtue of their hackles only as long as the latter stay dry. There are various floatants which can be applied to the fly and which will keep it riding high and dry for prolonged periods. I have tried most of them, but have settled on *Mucilin* as the most dependable.

Now, at long last, let's move on to the actual fishing.

As already pointed out, it is necessary to fish upstream to get a realistic float of the fly. Other things being equal, the ideal position is one from which the cast is not made directly upstream, but at an upstream angle which quarters across the current. This lets the fly float over the trout while line and leader remain off to one side.

Once the cast has been made you must now take steps which are new to your experience. As fly, line and leader drift back toward you, you must take up the slack as it accumulates. This can give trouble unless the line is kept under control.

Line held like this can be controlled by merely tightening or relaxing fingers.

As can be seen from the illustration, the trick is to hold the line with the rod hand so that it comes *up* between the first and second finger, and *down* between the second and third. (This is a very important "hold," invaluable while playing a fish, setting the hook or whenever else a solid pull is needed.) Control of the line is now complete: Relax the fingers and the line runs freely; squeeze them slightly and the effect is that of a light brake; squeeze them tightly and the line is immediately snubbed tight.

Secure the line in this manner as soon as the cast is completed. If you have rod and line in the right hand, reach forward with the left hand and grasp the line just below where it emerges from between the fingers of the right hand. A downward sweep of the arm will now strip in nearly 3 feet of line. Continue stripping line as required, holding the accumulated line in coils, preparatory for recasting.

The goal, of course, is to maintain as tight or straight a line as possible in order to set the hook instantly when a trout takes the fly.

Speed of reaction is important, for although a trout may be fooled into taking a fly for the real thing visually, it realizes its mistake instantly the moment it takes the fly in its mouth. Apart from the rarest exceptions, it retains the fly for no more than a split second, and it is in this tiny interval that you must react if you are to set the hook.

Since the leader tippet must be wispy in the interest of deception, both speed and delicacy must be incorporated in the act if you are to hook the fish without breaking the leader. A too hard yank, by the way, will break a tippet against a seven-inch trout as easily as against a trout of twice that length.

The right combination of speed and restraint is a tough thing to learn. After many years of dry fly fishing, I, for one, am still learning—or trying to. But more often than I like to admit I still manage to ruin an otherwise perfect production by breaking off a good fish on the take. Usually it's because I let myself get caught napping. Trout, doggone 'em, seem to take advantage of such moments deliberately!

I remember such an instance which took place on the Castleton River in southwestern Vermont. The stream is small, but at the time it held many brook trout, plus a lesser number of large browns.

I was fishing a stretch where the stream had cut high, vertical banks, much too high for me to see over. A really large trout had risen just upstream from me, and I was watching breathlessly as my fly floated toward him, when a large object hurtled across the stream, only a few feet above my head. Startled, I glanced up to see a lone black duck disappearing at jet speed. Quickly, I looked at my fly, but too late—or so I thought. The fly was gone and in its place swirled a mighty turbulence.

Disregarding restraint in what I mistakenly thought was a need for extra speed, I set the hook with a hefty yank. As it turned out, I had all the time in the world, for the big trout had retained the fly longer than usual as larger trout sometimes do. The hook bit home, but the leader parted. And once again trout fishing handed me that unique sense of frustation which comes of catastrophe for which you can blame only yourself.

The problem of hook setting did not arise during your downstream wet fly fishing for when trout hit a fly against a tight line they either hook themselves, or fail to do so, before the fisherman can do anything about it. In dry fly fishing they almost never hook themselves; the fisherman in this case must tighten his line against the trout. Applying just the right touch is one of the fine skills of the game, and if I had important advice to offer I would first follow it myself. A short rod should cut down the force and speed of the hook-setting yank, but I seem to be able to break off as many fish with a 6-ft. rod as with an 8-footer.

If a dry fly fisherman could have his choice, he would undoubtedly pick a time to fish when trout were rising to a hatch of mayflies. It is quite possible, however, to have fine dry fly fishing when no flies are hatching but when trout are hungry and surface minded.

It is in such "blind" dry fly fishing that knowledge gained concerning the likely whereabouts of trout in a stream can be used to great advantage. The challenge is not that of casting accurately and delicately to spots which experience leads you to believe hold unseen trout.

To come at the game without previous experience at this point would tend to make it appear to be a hopeless proposition. To the uninitiated, unless trout are showing at the surface, trout streams usually look completely fishless. The details of the bottom are clearly visible, except in the deepest pool, yet nowhere can one spot so much as a single trout.

Having already done a bit of trout fishing, you have learned that the inability to see trout in a stream is never true evidence of their absence. Confidence in your ability to deduce the whereabouts of unseen trout will grow as you do more and more blind dry fly fishing, and become increasingly skilled at "reading" the water. Careful, perceptive fishing will produce more and more strikes, and you will come to realize gradually that the number of trout in a given stream is generally underestimated.

I have known fishermen who restricted their trout fishing to only the first few weeks of the season, firm in their belief that in that short period the army of early season anglers had reduced the trout population to numbers too small to bother with. This is always a gross misconception. Trout fishing doesn't get really good until after a majority of the early season fishermen have lost interest. Even when trout fishing becomes difficult during the hottest months it is seldom due to a scarcity of trout.

This last has been borne out in recent years, during which trout seasons have been extended into the fall. Fishermen who take advantage of these extensions often enjoy some of the best dry fly fishing of the season, for the cool nights and crisp days seem to reawaken streams from their summer doldrums.

No, to cling to the belief that trout streams are fished out annually takes half the fun out of fishing. Instead, try to fish with the conviction that trout are there! You'll increase your enjoyment, and catch more trout, for the simple reason that in the majority of instances you will be right!

I have many fond memories of trout fishing, and in them all the accepted methods of trout fishing play important roles. I remember with much pleasure the heavy creels of worm-caught trout I have toted out from black fly infested bogs and beaver flowages when I was a young beginner at the game in northeastern Vermont. I still thrill to the recollections of the wild spin fishing I had shortly after World War II. Canoes, bush pilots and the strident cry of the loon are intermingled with my memories of sleek wilderness brook trout taken on wet flies and streamers in dozens of Maine ponds and streams.

But all such memories revolve around a solid core of dry fly fishing; what must add to hundreds of days on dozens and dozens of streams in Maine, New Hampshire and Vermont: Battenkill, Otter Creek, White, Lamoille, Moose, Kennebec, Baker, Connecticut, Clyde . . . —the list could go on and on.

All parts must be included in any sum total, of course, but I'm convinced that dry fly fishing is the one condiment which brings out the full and true flavor of New England trout fishing. Or maybe it's the other way around; perhaps it takes the shrewd sophistication of New England trout to bring out the full flavor of dry fly fishing.

In any event, I hope that those who are just beginning will find in dry fly fishing the fascination which it has held for me for, lo, these many years!

6

WET FLY FISHING, PHASE II

If it seemed logical to me to split wet fly fishing into two parts, it is perhaps because my own progress as a fly fisherman followed this pattern exactly.

While still very young I was drawn to fly fishing if for no other reason than to gain what was then the fly fisherman's exalted status among anglers. Fly fishing in those days consisted almost entirely of the brand of wet fly fishing discussed in Phase I. I was doing my fly fishing at that level when I first learned of dry fly fishing, and I succumbed instantly to its romantic appeal and to what I imagined to be its prestige-winning qualities.

It wasn't until my emotionally based zeal was replaced by a more sensible attitude that I came to realize that I had barely scratched the surface of wet fly fishing, and that it included a technique which is the most demanding test of a fly fisherman's skill.

As we have seen, the use of the wet fly as an excitement-arousing offering demands only rudimentary skill and it is therefore an ideal starting point for the beginning fisherman. The same wet fly, despite its lack of resemblance to any known item of trout food, can, nevertheless, be used in an imitative ploy. It is its use in this role which requires fly fishing skill of the highest order.

In the chapter devoted to trout nature and habits it was pointed out that the various stages and species of aquatic insect life form what is by far the bulk of the food which trout eat. Their feeding is the most noticeable, of course, when they are rising to take duns at the surface; it is therefore tempting to assume that their major interest is in "flies." Actually, insects in the winged stage are available to trout only during the moments of a hatch. They could hardly subsist on insects if these were the only periods of availability. Quite to the contrary, trout depend upon the nymphs and larvae of such insects for the major portion of their sustenance. These are available to them, on the bottoms of streams, lakes and ponds, every day of the year.

Thus, while the dry fly may seem to the fisherman to imitate that which is the trout's chief food, a little reflection will reveal that this cannot possibly be so. Much more representative of their total fare are imitations of the winged insects' nymphal or larval forms.

This imitation can be achieved by using artificials made to resemble actual nymphs as closely as possible. It can also be done indirectly by using standard wet flies. Although far from faithful reproductions, these flies, when fished along the bottom, at least suggest as affiliation with the nymphal form of insect life.

Except for those periods immediately following a hatch, trout stomachs invariably contain a quantity of nymphs and larvae. Mixed with these is what appears to be a conglomeration of debris from the stream bottom. The reason, undoubtedly, is that hiding nymphs must be scrounged from under rocks and from gravel and silt, and while ingesting the dislodged nymphs trout also ingest extraneous material inadvertently. Thus, while at their bottom scrounging, trout do not hesitate to grab anything that looks the least bit edible if it is borne along naturally by the current. This probably explains why they will pounce on a tumbling wet fly, even though it does not resemble a live nymph in appearance.

Nymphs can crawl and cling, but when dislodged they are at the mercy of the current. To imitate their "drift" with a wet fly it is obvious that we must cast upstream as in dry fly fishing. It is equally important to try to achieve a dragless drift while also attempting to keep the fly as close to the bottom as possible. This, believe me, is a mighty hard trick to pull off.

A bit of lead in the body of the fly, or added to the leader, would take the fly down certainly. But live nymphs are not made of lead, and trout, as you must have guessed by now, are immediately suspicious of lead-bodied imitations. But even if you succeed in sinking an unweighted wet fly to near the bottom, the problem of drag is now three dimensional. In other words, a sunken fly is acted upon by currents which not only may conflict horizontally, as upon the surface, but vertically as well. The trout, you can be sure, are as defensively attuned to violations of ascending and descending currents as to violations of those which act laterally.

The capsule which contains it is small, but the problem is a big one.

It is so tough, in fact, that many fly fishermen never attempt to solve it and many of those who do become discouraged after a few tries.

I tend to be stubborn, and at one time I stuck at it until I became fairly proficient. I have long since quit, however. So much has to be done by *feel*, and even *instinct*, that it's altogether too much like fishing blindfolded to suit me. It is unfortunate that the technique is open to this objection, for it goes straight to the heart of trout vulnerability. There are many times when trout are not surface minded and when dry fly fishing is all but futile. Neither can you excite trout with hardware, wet flies or streamers when the fish have been rendered sluggish by unfavorable water temperatures or other adverse conditions. But I think that it is safe to say that *always*, in every trout stream in the country, at least a few trout are nudging the bottom here and there, pecking about for tidbits and taking in any which come to their attention. Thus, while all other methods are appropriate only during certain periods and under certain conditions, dead-drift wet fly fishing, or nymph fishing if you prefer, is *always* logical and appropriate.

I stumbled upon the inherent appeal of a drifted and sunken wet fly quite by accident, many years ago. I was young, cocky and quite certain that I already knew all there was to know about wet fly fishing *and* dry fly fishing.

I was exploring a small stream that was new to me in the vicinity of Montpelier. The section I was checking out was a series of long, shallow pools, the water crystal clear and the flow relatively light. I was fishing downstream, casting a wet fly ahead of me and skittering it back in what I then held to be the only way to fish a wet fly. I couldn't stir up a single strike, but to my great consternation good-sized trout fled ahead of me each time I waded down through a just-fished pool. Although I tried to work my wet fly as enticingly as possible, I covered at least a quarter-mile of stream without catching a single trout.

When it came time to return to my car, I couldn't put out of mind all those trout I had spooked. Instead of quitting the stream, I reversed my direction and began casting the same wet fly upstream. I had no substantial hopes, however, for I had long been conditioned to the belief that the only productive way to fish a wet fly was downstream.

The horizons of my fishing world were soon to broaden, however, for after casting to the head of one of the long pools I thought I distinguished the hint of a flash beneath the spot where my fly had landed and sunk. I struck instinctively and, to my astonishment and delight, I felt the rod bow against a good fish.

The experience was so innovative in the light of my experience that I immediately took time out for reflection. I was certain that the trout had taken the wet fly at a moment when I was not agitating it, when, in fact, *it was doing nothing but sinking and drifting!* Was this merely a fluke, or had I discovered an unsuspected facet of wet fly appeal? Furthermore, I had neither felt the strike nor had I actually seen it. I had set the hook at what was nothing more than a mere hint of action. Had the whole thing fallen together by coincidence and luck, culminating in a long-shot result that I couldn't hope to duplicate? We would see.

The limit in those days was a generous twenty trout. Also, by the standards of the time, a man would have been looked upon as a fool if he deliberately quit short of his limit, or if he returned legal trout to the stream. So, when I left the stream with a creel stuffed to the brim with rainbows, browns and brookies, it was with a clear conscience and a sense of elation that was almost dizzying.

Time after time I had carried off successfully, as my heavy creel testified, a series of steps which, by the light of previous convictions, should have added to nothing: an upstream cast; deep down strikes that barely could be sensed; setting the hook almost by guesswork. Unorthodox to the point of heresy. Yet there was no denying the shoulder-sagging creel and the twenty fat trout which it contained!

Discoveries made by independent effort are heady triumphs. It was probably the smug feeling of having pried open the door to a major secret that turned my enthusiasm to upstream fishing with wet flies and nymphs for several seasons thereafter. I discovered the day-to-day efficacy of the technique. I learned the necessity of keeping the fly as close to the bottom as possible, and the trick of taking advantage of all plunging currents to achieve this aim. I learned to detect strikes, not only by watching for the flash or flicker of the fish as it took, but by keeping my eye fastened on my floating line for a momentary halt or check. I learned that striking at the slightest provocation was a dandy way to hook sunken logs, rocks and even old automobile tires. But I also learned that in a surprisingly high percentage of instances the cause of the line's check was a trout which had taken the fly unseen.

As I have already stated, my enthusiasm for this kind of fly fishing has waned, largely because most of the visual thrills which I so enjoy in dry fly fishing are lacking. My respect for the high order of angling skill which it requires has not diminished; if anything, it has grown. My hat is off to the fisherman who takes his trout by this method, for he has to be the most skillful of all fly fishermen.

Furthermore, I will say this much for the attending thrills. There is no greater sense of triumph than that which comes of driving the hook into a fish that you only half believed was there!

I did my upstream wet fly fishing with exactly the same floating line and tapered leader that I used for dry fly fishing. If I were to have another go at it today, I would rig up for it in exactly the same way. There are now sinking fly lines that would take the fly down quickly, and there are floating lines with sinking tips. I would fear excessive drag from the sunken line, or sunken portion of line, and I know I would be partially lost without a floating line to help me sense strikes.

A notable exception would be that of fishing wet flies and nymphs at the bottoms of ponds and lakes. Here there is no problem of drag, for there are no currents. Consequently, the natural action which must be imitated is not the uninhibited drift of a dislodged nymph or larva, but the crawling progress of the live insect. A sinking line is a must in this instance, for the nymph imitation must inch along the bottom in order to be convincing.

This type of fishing can be very effective, by the way, if the fisherman adopts the theory that he cannot fish his lure too slowly. A very slow "hand twist" retrieve will cause the nymph imitation to creep along the bottom where it will come to the attention of any trout in the vicinity.

The hand twist retrieve consists of rocking the line-holding hand first one way and then the other, each "rock" gathering in the short span of line stretching across the four fingers. Frequent pauses, and slight twitches of the rod, will enhance the lifelike effect.

The reader has undoubtedly seen many references to nymph fishing as a fly fishing method which stands apart from all others, but there is little difference between it and wet fly fishing when the wet fly is used to imitate nymphs. Both the wet fly and the artificial nymph will achieve identical results when fished so as to tumble with the current, as close to the bottom as possible.

The fly fisherman who delves into the method—all should at least give it a try, if only for edification—can benefit by turning over a few rocks in trout streams and examining the nymphs which can be seen clinging to the undersides of the rocks. While exact imitation is by no means necessary, their common drabness of color should be heeded when selecting wet flies. Gaudy patterns such as Royal Coachman, Parmachene Belle and Yellow Sally would be illogical choices while such patterns as Quill Gordon, Dark Hendrickson and Leadwing Coachman are much more in keeping with the natural color scheme.

Direct imitations of nymphs can be purchased or tied, of course, although it is very difficult to turn out faithful reproductions of live nymphs

Hand twist retrieve imitates slow crawl of live nymph.

at the tying vise—or to turn out *really convincing* imitations of anything, for that matter. Fishermen tend to accord perfection to any fly which conforms to the notion of what that particular *pattern* should look like, without serious regard for the degree to which it resembles the live insect which is supposedly its model. Any fly tier would undoubtedly risk censure who dared violate the traditional dressing of the Quill Gordon in order to achieve a more lifelike resemblance of *Iron Frauditor,* the species of mayfly which the Quill Gordon was created to imitate.

Fortunately, trout seem as easily (?) fooled by approximation as by exact similarity, and pattern in upstream wet fly fishing is not of great importance. But here, as in dry fly fishing, size *is* important.

While it is true that the larvae and nymphs of some aquatic insects reach considerable size, and are snapped up eagerly by trout (the hellgrammite is one example), my experience in trying to lure large trout with large nymph imitations has been uniformly disappointing. I suspect that it is because it is very difficult, if not impossible, to fish the oversize artificials convincingly.

Flies and nymphs in sizes 10, 12 and 14 seem to be the most reliable producers, with the edge going to the smallest of these, if there is any. The same inverse relationship exists with respect to the amount of dressing; the sparser the latter, short of a bare hook, of course, the better the trout seem to like it. In fact, where the current is exceptionally slow, and in ponds and lakes, a few turns of material on a No. 16 hook, with a wisp of hackle for a tail, is often especially deadly. The body material can be anything that can be wound on, or bound down, to give a segmental appearance.

Upstream wet fly fishing, or nymph fishing, is a phase of fly fishing which most experienced fly fishermen cede to be deadly—and then ignore. I can't say that I blame them. But please be advised that nymph fishing's reputation is no myth; it is a deadly method, but one which is difficult to master.

If you do master it, you will be able to take trout as long as any remain in our streams, ponds and lakes. And if you happen to be a person who takes pride in doing things the hard way, you can bask in the knowledge that there is no harder way to take trout!

7

FISHING FOR LAKE TROUT

The lake trout, or *togue* as he's called in Maine, is an altogether different critter from the rainbow, the brown and the brook trout. Standard trout fishing methods are largely useless in his pursuit, his capture requiring tackle and strategy quite outside the stream fisherman's experience.

Yet no book devoted to New England trout fishing could claim completeness without a chapter devoted to the laker for the lake trout is rare to waters of the United States. The fact that the species exists in certain New England lakes, and thus affords angling of a rather exotic nature, is sufficient to justify discussion.

The lake trout is a fish of comparative mystery, insofar as tracing its origin and accounting for its distribution are concerned.

Our present-day trout are generally believed to have originated in arctic seas and then, during the last ice age, to have moved southward ahead of the great ice sheets. When the ice finally retreated, trout became landlocked in the lakes and streams which the ice left in its wake. The original distribution of the other trout species seems to tie in nicely with this theory, but certain irregularities in the distribution of the lake trout seem to defy explanation, thus leaving its evolution and history open to debate and speculation.

In any event, the lake trout is the most discriminatory of all trout when it comes to habitat. It simply cannot tolerate high, or even moderate, water temperatures. In the deep lakes, which are its only New England haunts, it rises to near the surface only briefly, directly after ice-out, and retreats, usually to great depths, as soon as the surface temperature rises significantly.

Its sensitivity to warm water exceeds even that of the landlocked salmon. Although the salmon seek relief in the depths when lake waters warm near the top, they are to be found the year around in certain Maine streams which remain relatively cold. Lake trout, if found in New England streams at all, are found there only briefly during early spring while the water is still icy.

Lakers are not averse to streams *per se.* In the Canadian subarctic they live the year around in rivers whose waters remain in the forties during the brief summers. There they will rise to wet flies, streamers and other trout lures fished on or near the surface, which usually comes as a surprise to fishermen familiar with only the New England variety of the species.

The lake trout is not a spectacular fighter when hooked, but it has it all over other eastern trout when it comes to size. Specimens weighing over twenty pounds are caught each year in the lakes of Maine, New Hampshire and Vermont. Fish of that size, even though not noted for their fighting qualities, must be treated with respect and care if they are to be landed.

On a salmon fishing trip to the George River in northern Quebec, I was surprised to have lakers, weighing up to ten pounds, latch onto my flies in the fast water where I fished for salmon. The fishing camp was located where the river broadened to form a lake, and I asked the proprietor about the lake trout that might inhabit that likelier looking water.

"Only one party ever tried for them deliberately," he said. "They trolled deep with big spoons and caught four fish which weighed a hundred and twenty pounds!

"I tried it once," he added. "I was using fifty-pound test line and busted it on the first fish I hooked!"

Unlike other trout, the laker shows little or no interest in insects. In New England lakes the lake trout subsist almost entirely on smelt, and it is only in lakes which have substantial populations of these small fish that lake trout are to be found.

In early spring, lake trout are taken inadvertently by fishermen trolling for salmon with streamers and small spoons and wobblers. Their stay near the surface is brief, and once they go down the fisherman must fish his lure at their level, 50 feet or more below the surface, if he is to succeed.

Such deep fishing poses serious problems and forces unattractive compromises. As a result, only a few dedicated fishermen fish seriously and steadily for lake trout.

I can understand why. With the assistance and advice of Cret MacArthur, a guide who knows the bottom of Maine's West Grand Lake as he

Lake trout make up in size for whatever fighting qualities they may lack.

knows the bottom of his canoe, I spent an entire day dragging bottom in nearly a hundred feet of water and never got a strike.

Dedicated lake trout fishermen have to be a special breed, one which can tolerate long periods of monotonous, fruitless trolling that would drive most men to distraction. Lake Dunmore, which is only a few miles from my home in Pittsford, Vermont, still holds a few lakers. They are *mighty* few, however, and the time between strikes tends to be enormous. Nevertheless, at least one local fisherman fishes the lake enthusiastically all season long. I doubt if he catches more than a half-dozen lakers a year, but his biggest fish last summer weighed fourteen pounds!

As the reader probably has deduced, I am neither an enthusiastic lake trout fisherman nor one qualified to pass out advice except perhaps at the most elementary level. I have caught lake trout in Maine, Vermont, Labrador and Quebec, but as often by accident as by design. I can honestly lay claim to but little savvy when it comes to fishing for them seriously and deliberately. What follows is submitted only with the intent of helping to get off on the right foot those to whom the prospect of lake trout fishing has strong appeal.

If you happen to be one of those, you will undoubtedly need to acquire the specialized tackle which lake trout fishing requires.

In the old days, lake trout fishermen used heavily weighted silk lines to reach the necessary depths. Then came lines of single strand copper, braided copper and monel wire, in that order. The single strand copper line would take lures down quickly, and to great depths, but it was tricky stuff to use—a kink while playing a fish was usually fatal. Lines of braided copper had less tendency to kink, but their greater bulk and resistance detracted from their sinking quality. Today, monel metal lines are usually used whenever the fish are more than 50 feet down. It is much more trustworthy than the old copper lines, but like any wire line it is unpleasant to handle.

A fourth innovation, the lead core line, has largely solved the handling problem. For those who may not know, a lead core line is a braided fabric line with a soft lead core to make it sink quickly. Because of its fabric exterior it has much the feel of a fly line of the same diameter, and it handles—spools in and pays out—almost as easily. It does not have the wire line's tendency to kink and a kink is not fatal if one should develop.

These lead core lines are made for trolling, of course. They come in hundred-yard lengths. Each ten yards is dyed a distinctive color to enable the fisherman to pay out any desired length of line by simply counting the colors as they come off the reel.

The depth achieved by a given length of line is not constant, of course.

It depends on the trolling speed and the resistance set up by the lure being trolled. With experience, however, fishermen learn how many colors to pay out to take a small lure to a given depth, and how many more colors to let out to take a larger lure to the same depth.

Unfortunately, the lead core line will not take lures much deeper than fifty feet, and lines of monel wire are generally used whenever there is a need to go deeper.

Old timers had to learn the contours of the bottom by sounding (and snagging!) in various locations, but technology has eliminated this chore. Well-equipped lake trout fishermen now rely on electronic sounding equipment to keep them informed of the depth at all times. I have had no experience with such devices, but they cannot be other than invaluable.

Space is lacking for an in-depth discussion of water stratification, but the bottom stratum, while coldest, is likely to be stagnant. The stratum in which suitable temperatures and sufficient oxygen are combined may lie considerably above the bottom, save in those places where reefs rise up and penetrate this sustaining area. These spots are favored by lake trout, spots where they can constantly inspect the bottom while enjoying comfortable temperatures and abundant oxygen. The depth of this fish-holding stratum (thermocline) can be determined with the help of a thermometer, for it is a relatively thin layer in which the temperature drops sharply in but a few feet of descent. This known, the depth finder can be used to determine all reefs which lie within the thermocline, and it is there that the lake trout are almost certain to be.

The lake trout is pikelike in its predatory habits, and lures which will take northern pike and pickerel will take lakers. These include the Dardevle, Flatfish, Record Spoon, Rapala, Mooselook and the like. These should be fished on a level leader at least six feet long. Leaders should be rugged, but of less test than the line in order to prevent line breakage when bottom-snagged lures must be broken off. Swivels of the best quality should be used between line and leader and between leader and lure. This need for double precaution arises from the continuous trolling and its tendency to twist leader and line.

When using plugs, spoons and wobblers it is customary to liven the action by either pumping the line with the rod or by holding the line in hand and swinging the arm over the side to cause the lure to spurt ahead and then fall back. If the line is hand held, fish are played from the rod after hooking, of course.

A traditional lure for lake trout consists of a single spinner and a "sewn" smelt or chub. The spinner, which acts as an attractor, should precede the bait by a couple of feet.

69

A smelt or chub is sewn on a hook in order to make it spin slowly as it is trolled. This is one instance where a snelled hook is to be preferred because of the absence of an eye which would make it difficult to draw the hook through the bait. To sew on a bait, proceed as follows: run the point of the hook *down* through the lower lip. Draw the hook clear, plus several inches of snell. Run the hook *down* through the top of the head and pull clear once more. Finally slide the barb of the hook under the skin at a point halfway between dorsal fin and tail. Point the barb toward the tail as it enters the skin, but rotate the hook so that the barb will point toward the head of the bait when it emerges. Now, by adjusting the snell at the first two punctures, the body of the bait can be drawn into a curve which will cause it to spin slowly when trolled.

In fishing a sewn bait behind a spinner no action is imparted by the fisherman other than that produced by the steady pace of the fishing craft.

Getting a deep trolling rig into operation is quite a chore, and the temptation to leave well enough alone is strong, once it seems to be at the proper depth and apparently working properly. Even though all seems to be going well, it pays to check every so often. During prolonged trolling it is all too easy for the bait to pick up a twig or leaf from the lake floor, foul itself on the leader or render itself ineffectual in some other way. It is always embarrassing to discover that several strikeless hours *may* have been due to just such a "discombobulation" which you took no pains to discover and rectify.

Perhaps the most effective lake trout fishing device of all, but one which is an abomination to use, is the Dave Davis rig. This consists of several spinner blades in tandem and is fished ahead of a sewn bait, nightcrawlers or an artificial lure. The spinner blade nearest the fisherman is usually king-sized with the rest diminishing in size in the direction of the bait or lure.

The blades serve as attractors, rather than actual lures, giving off an enormous amount of reflected light which calls lakers to where they notice the bait and take it, of course, if all works well. On a calm day, in the clear water of northern trout lakes, the descent of this device can be followed to great depths by its flash and glitter.

Needless to say, the Dave Davis rig, often referred to as *cow bells*, sets up great resistance as it churns through the water. This requires the use of a very stiff rod which, with the drag of the hardware, greatly cuts down the action and thrills normally associated with playing hooked fish. None, save the largest of lake trout, can give good accounts of themselves when forced to drag around a collection of spoons while fighting for their lives. Consequently, although the Dave Davis rig enjoys some popularity because of its effectiveness, most sports-minded fishermen choose not to use it.

Lake trout trolling outfits usually consist of a short, stiff rod of the type often called "boat rods" and a reel capable of holding the required amount of wire or lead line. The amount of line needed will vary from lake to lake, depending on the depth of the trout holding stratum. The reel should hold enough line to take lures to the desired depth, plus a nominal amount of reserve or backing. Many lake trout fishermen prefer multiplying reels of the type used for light salt-water fishing. Many others, possibly more, like the simplicity of operation of big-spool, single action reels made especially for wire line trolling. The Pflueger "Sal-Trout" is an old favorite; the Pflueger "Pakron" is designed for the same job but comes equipped with additional features and refinements.

An outfit such as described above is, without question, the most practical one for deep trolling. Again without question, it detracts greatly from the fun of using light tackle. This can be avoided to a considerable degree, however, if the fisherman doesn't mind substituting one set of compromises for another.

In my case, as an example, I get around the heavy tackle bit by using stainless steel wire of only .009 inch diameter. An enormous length can be wound on an ordinary fly reel. If you pay out enough of this line it will take streamers and small metal lures to great depths.

This fine line creates very little resistance when trolled. It would be possible to use it on a fly rod. For a bit more stiffness, however, I mount my wire-filled fly reel on a spinning rod with free sliding rings so that the reel can be mounted at the rear of the grip as on a fly rod.

That's the good news; now for the bad. The thin wire line tests only 8 lbs. It will kink if not handled with unrelenting care, and a kink reduces its strength to practically zero. Finally, an excessive amount of line must be payed out to attain substantial depth.

Nevertheless, I have used this line successfully to take lakers and landlocked salmon from deep water in the summer months. Strikes come as electrifying jolts (true of all wire line fishing) for there is no stretch to the line and the rod must absorb the full force of the hit. Then begins a battle, beginning hundreds of feet astern, during which one kink over the entire give-and-take spells catastrophe.

If this sounds exciting, which it is, be advised that getting maybe 400 feet of fine wire into production, without kink or snarl, is no small chore. Then, all too often, the lure snags on a reef just as you think you're in production. All that line yardage has to be backed down through the guides and onto the reel, the lure unstuck if possible, and then the whole tedious paying out process gone through again. This is no joy at any time, but on windy days when jockeying boat or canoe is particularly difficult it can become downright exasperating.

I'm sure that the reader has percieved that I have written this chapter from a position with respect to lake trout fishing that is something less than enthusiastic. While this may be true, I have nothing but respect for those who are willing to endure the tedium of hours of futile trolling for a single strike from a big fish. To be truthful, I envy their patience and perseverance. I'd like to boat a walloping big laker now and then myself, but, unlike them, I lack the required fortitude and stoicism.

Despite my personal shortcomings, I urge my readers to give lake trout fishing a try, at the very least. For one thing, you may be one of the minority who finds its unique challenge altogether to your liking. Even if you do not, you have not savored the full flavor of New England trout fishing until you have caught at least one lake trout. To ignore the opportunity is to miss out on something special that the region has to offer.

8
TACKLE AND EQUIPMENT

In my last year's Christmas list of wanted items, I included "a glass fly rod, the cheapest you can find." During the course of a fishing season I do a considerable amount of bait fishing for a wide variety of species, and I don't relish the idea of risking expensive fly rods against such critters as 15-lb. catfish, brutally powerful bowfins, big northern pike and an assortment of other fish.

My son obliged, informing me at the time of presentation that he had followed my instruction concerning cost to the letter. Despite the fact that the rod had cost only a few dollars, I could recall, after putting the two sections together, when rods of such pleasant feel, lightness and strength were not available at any price. At least, if they were, I never got *my* hands on one!

As with all cheap rods, certain corners had been cut. There were too few guides; the windings needed additional coats of varnish; ferrules and reel seat were from the bottom of the heap. But the rod was straight and true, with the feel of plenty of built-in power despite full sensitivity. Add a few guides and it would be a fly rod that no fly fisherman would have serious grounds to complain about.

I have used the foregoing example to try to make the point that past generations of fishermen had to make do with little, most of which was highly unsuitable. In my own case, I'm convinced that the trout I managed to catch as a youth were caught despite the tackle I had to use, rather than because of it. None but the present generation of beginning trout fishermen has ever had such a wealth of tackle to choose from.

It would be easy to write about the present-day abundance of tackle from a position of neutrality, cataloging the bulk of that which is available without designating items of superior quality. It will be much harder to name names and make choices, but it seems to me that this must be my policy if I am to be of any help to the beginner, or possibly to others as well.

Although I intend to recommend to the best of my ability and judgment, it should be obvious that no one fisherman could come close to testing all the brands of equipment currently on the market. I shall not hesitate to recommend by name those items which have given me long and satisfactory service, but, in most cases, as the best in my experience; not to the exclusion of all else.

The foregoing chapters have dealt with the various techniques and methods of trout fishing, each of which requires specific items of equipment. Discussion of tackle was intentionally omitted at the time in order to concentrate utterly on the matter of luring trout. Now, let's go over the same field again, but this time from the standpoint of suitable tackle and gear. Bait fishing came first, so we shall start there.

Due to the spinning outfit's widespread popularity, spinning reels and rods see much service in bait fishing for trout. In general, however, the spinning rig is quite unsuitable for the job, the only exception being the ultralight outfit and its ability to cast tiny, light baits. Otherwise the spinning reel is a handicap in bait fishing, mainly because the spinning reel denies the fisherman the instant line control which is vital.

A fly rod and single action reel are much better suited to the needs. Line can be released *the instant* the need arises, and only this facility, plus the fly rod's sensitivity, permits the fishing of natural bait with the most telling effect.

As indicated at the beginning of this chapter, a glass fly rod which will make an excellent bait fishing rod can be bought for only a few dollars. One of the richest sources of such rods, and of certain items of basic equipment at rock-bottom prices, is the sporting goods sections of big department stores. Another is the mail-order houses which advertise regularly in the outdoor magazines: Netcraft, Finnysport, Herter's and Cabela's are just a few. These companies specialize in do-it-yourself components and in the basic needs of the fisherman. Their prices are reasonable and their catalogs are fascinating.

As already noted, a cheap glass fly rod is almost certain to need more guides. I just counted the guides on a couple of my fly rods. A 7½-footer has nine guides, counting the top; an 8-footer sports a total of ten. My under-the-Christmas-tree "cheapie" came rigged with only five.

Good line control is needed for serious bait fishing, so the smart thing to do is to remove the existing guides to permit respacing, and increase the total to the number found on first quality fly rods of the same length.

Winding on guides is not difficult, and can be a pleasant way to spend a cold winter evening. For a smooth job, start the winding on the rod, then bring it up over the foot of the guide. (Hold the guide in place while making the first wind by taping the other foot to the rod with scotch tape.) Wind a separate loop of thread under the last five of six turns. Run the end of the winding thread through the eye of the loop and draw it under those last few windings by pulling the loop free. Trim with a sharp knife or razor blade. For a fuzz-free varnish job, singe each winding by passing it quickly through the flame of a candle.

Start winding on rod, then bring up over foot of guide (note tape securing guide).

One important thing to remember is that it takes several coats of varnish, as many as five, to cover the windings completely. This last must be done or exposed windings will wear through quickly, come unwound and leave you with the job to do all over. When completely covered by spar varnish, windings will last for years.

There is an old saying that you get about what you pay for, and, for the most part, it is even more true of fishing tackle than of all else. However, once you add the needed guides and varnish to a cheap glass rod you do not have an inferior product for the simple reason that virtually *all* glass rod sections, expensive or cheap, are basically of good quality. Action can be modified by changes in design, of course, but the basic material is always tough and reliable, as good for bait fishing as that found in much more expensive rods.

If good rods can be bought cheaply, how about reels? Here, alas, the old adage of getting what you pay for asserts itself with a vengeance. It is tempting to spend only three or four dollars on a single action reel which *looks* well made and reliable and which seems to perform satisfactorily in the store. Unfortunately, reels come in for a tremendous amount of wear and tear, and cheap reels simply can't stand the gaff. They invariably wear out, or fall apart, long before you've had your money's worth and usually at a critical moment.

Pflueger Medalist: Author's choice as best for the money.
Pflueger.

When it comes to single action fly reels, for bait fishing *and* fly fishing, the biggest bargain known to me is the Pflueger "Medalist." It is available in a variety of sizes to suit all needs (the #1494 is my choice here and for general fly fishing) and it has features which to my mind are superior to the counterparts of much more expensive reels. One is the click, an ingenious arrangement which works only half as hard when line is wound in as when it is paid out. In my opinion it is much better and certainly more durable than the spring-and-dog clicks found in most reels and which have held up my fishing by breaking just when the fish were hungriest.

The second feature is the drag, which in the Medalist is highly func-
tional. I have several expensive English reels, and in these the drags are
little better than affectations since the difference in tension is hardly noticeable between full on or completely off. Not so with the Medalist. The
drag is thoroughly businesslike, adjustable from no tension at all to no-go
finality when screwed tight. This reel sells for around $14.00 from the
competetive supply houses, little more than one-third the price of the
highly touted English reels.

When monofilament line first became available I thought it would
make an ideal line for stream bait fishing, but it proved to be a disappoint-
ment. It cut visibility to a minimum, of couse, but it lacked sufficient bulk
and body for proper manipulation. I have used old double tapered fly lines,
but these are *too* bulky, save toward the tip. On the other hand, the
running portion of forward taper fly lines are excellent, for they are of the
right diameter and usually remain in good condition after the forward
taper has lost its finish. Lacking this source, an F Level fly line is an exact
duplicate.

Leaders for most bait fishing need be only three to four feet in length,
of level monofilament in 6 to 8 lb. test. Here again, for basic nylon for level
leaders, trolling and routine spinning, I frequent the bargain counters of
the chain stores. Quarter-pound spools of monofilament, in various
weights, can be bought for little more than a dollar. The line is perfectly
satisfactory for all but the most demanding needs, so why pay more?

Finally, we come to the business end of the line and hooks and sinkers.
The best hooks cost so little that it is unwise to use anything else. Along
the banks of trout streams you will find a scattering of cardboard folders
which once held snelled hooks. These were dropped by fishermen who
were not only litterbugs, but poor judges of hooks. With a monofilament
leader, a snell serves no purpose but to add an unnecessary loop near the
hook.

The best Mustad hooks (unsnelled) can be bought from fly-tying supply houses for around $1.50 per hundred. Buy the type used for tying wet
flies: normal weight wire, turned down eye, hollow ground point, in sizes
4, 6, 8 and 10. For fishing very tiny baits such as caddis larvae and nymphs,
buy the same style hooks in light wire (designed for tying dry flies) in sizes
12 and 14. Tie these hooks directly to your leader with the Turle knot. Use
finer than usual leaders with the smallest hooks.

Hooks with rolled in points have become very popular for bait fishing,
probably not so much for any superior hooking qualities as for their
"claw" appearance which has strong sales appeal. Appearances to the
contrary, I prefer to pin my faith on a plain round bend—the "Model

Perfect" in fly-tying parlance—for I doubt that it has ever been exceeded for efficiency.

Sinkers are humble but necessary and important items. For most trout fishing you will need no more than one or two split BB's on your leader. In heavier water, a single split buckshot will usually suffice. Clamp sinkers to the leader about a foot above the bait. Always test after clamping, for this sometimes weakens the leader.

There are other bait fishing needs, of course, but since these apply to all trout fishing in general, we will deal with them collectively later.

Spin fishing, the next method covered, calls for a special reel, special rod, special line and lures designed especially for this type of fishing.

The first spinning reels to appear in this country were looked on as marvels of ingenuity, the stationary spool being hailed as the height of innovation. It seems hardly possible that the principle of the spinning reel is now taken for granted, and that spinning reels require no description in even the most basic of how-to-do-it texts. The world has indeed passed me by!

Best quality spinning reels sell for around $30.00, and from here the price drops to as low as only a few dollars. Like all reels, however, the spinning reel must stand up under much wear and tear, an excessive amount, in fact, for the spinning reel is in almost constant use throughout every fishing day. Cheap reels just won't take it, and it is false economy to buy them. You can also get hooked on expensive spinning reels if they are of complicated design, for their intricate innards are bound to go haywire.

I can't speak for or against *all* spinning reels, of course, for there are those which I have never used. Among the considerable number I *have* owned and used I have yet to find the equal of the Orvis 100 A. Remove the gear plate and you look in on a beautifully designed and machined worm drive—and little else. The construction is simplicity itself, with correspondingly little to go wrong. I have owned an Orvis 100 (original version of the 100 A) for nearly 20 years and in both fresh and salt water it has taken on such rugged scrappers as stripers, bluefish, bonito, arctic char, northern pike, lake trout, catfish, gar, bowfins to say nothing of rainbows, browns, brookies, landlocked salmon and a *potpourri* of other fresh water species. It has banged around in the bottoms of boats and canoes, in jeeps and in bush-hopping planes. As far as I can tell from its performance, it is as sound today as the day I bought it. I am certain that the service that this one reel has given would have eaten up a small fortune in the cost of cheap reels which turn out to be the most expensive in the long run.

Author's first choice of spinning reels.
The Orvis Company, Inc.

There are other reliable spinning reels, of course, but again I would warn the prospective buyer to insist on simplicity. No spinning reel is going to stand up if it is stuffed with coil springs, complicated cams and dozens of screws to work loose.

Quite probably I should make clear that in speaking of *spinning reels* I am referring to reels of open-face design and not to closed-face *spin cast reels*. The latter are designed to stand in for the bait casting reel, the multiplying, level wind reel used to cast plugs and other heavy lures for bass, pike, etc., and are unsatisfactory for the light spinning involved in trout fishing.

The action of the trout fishing spinning rod can fall anywhere within fairly broad limits, and is therefore not critical. A so-called "light" action is most suitable for tossing lures which weigh around ¼ oz., but the term is a loose one which embraces considerable variation. For that reason, as in the case of bait fishing fly rods, it is possible to buy a spinning rod for very little money which will give satisfactory service and stand up under long, hard usage.

The sources of such rods are exactly those named as sources of cheap fly rods. My son, noticing what seemed to be an unusual bargain in one of my catalogs, recently ordered a glass spinning rod offered for $5.00. The rod has proven to be perfectly adequate: good action, plenty of backbone and reasonably well constructed—an outstanding bargain.

The cheaper spinning rods usually have enough guides, but as should be expected, they are of poor quality. In time they will become line scored and will need replacing. Also, as in the case of inexpensive fly rods, the windings should be given additional coats of spar varnish for full protection. But basically, thanks to the consistency of glass, these economical spinning rods are sound and strong and will give long service.

However, if cost is of less concern than the ultimate in quality, the leading rod manufacturers offer truly elegant rods, in glass and bamboo, for correspondingly high prices. To me, the difference in action and construction is not worth the difference in cost. Spinning is just too coarse a form of casting for genuine appreciation of nth degree rod refinement. Others may disagree, while still others may get more than their money's worth just from pride of possession. More power to any and all of these persuasions!

I tend to favor rather short spinning rods, but this, within limits, is a matter of personal taste. I think that for trout fishing a spinning rod which is more than seven feet long would be a disadvantage, and most fishermen probably would be unhappy with a rod shorter than a six-footer.

Ultralight spinning was identified as a highly effective trout fishing method. Again, a top quality reel is the only sensible choice. The one I have used for years is a fine piece of equipment. Tiny and beautifully made, it is an Italian import which, to the best of my knowledge, is no longer available in this country. While there are many models and brands of conventional spinning reels, there is no such wide choice of ultralight reels. I can make only one recommendation in good conscience.

This spring I bought an Orvis 50 A, purely on the strength of my long service from the Orvis 100. This tiny reel, a miniature of the 100, promises to be every bit as satisfactory. I have not yet put it to the test of years, of course, but I have been delighted with its performance to date and I feel that its construction guarantees durability.

By way of general advice, certain features should be present in the ultralight spinning reel. Due to the small spool diameter, the retrieve ratio should be a least 5:1 to allow rapid reeling when necessary. Also, because lines as light as 2 lb. test will be used, the drag must be very sensitive and reliable. In other words, the drag should allow tension to be increased little by little until just the proper degree has been attained. Any lack of sensitivity or roughness in this department will cost you many a fish and cause you much grief.

In ultralight spinning, rod action *is* important, and this rules out bargain-basement economy. The glass rod which I have used for years is, like the reel, no longer available. This rod is 4½ ft. long and weighs around 1½ oz. The action is very soft, and carries over the entire length. This permits the casting of very light lures—and makes a foot-long trout feel like a leviathan!

Since I have done all my ultralight spinning with this one rod, I can make only general recommendations. I doubt that rods as short and light as mine are generally available, and it is probably true that the beginner would feel more comfortable with one a bit heavier and stiffer. My advice would be to select a five-foot rod recommended by the manufacturer for use with lures of 1/16 oz. to ¼ oz. glass if I had to count my money, or bamboo if I wanted to splurge.

Spinning lines, of any and all weights, are not easy to assess despite the fact that they all look pretty much alike. I have bought some that were relatively expensive, very strong for their diameter and splendid to cast, only to have them cost me good fish through undiscovered deterioration —undiscovered, that is, up to the moment of tragedy. I have bought cheap bulk monofilament that cast satisfactorily and stood up for long periods. This comes from the sloppy habit of buying indiscriminately.

I am therefore forced to confess that the only spinning line I *know* from experience to be easy to cast and thoroughly reliable is Garcia Platyl. Another of alleged superiority is Trilene, but I regret to say that I have never tried it.

Regardless of brand or alleged strength, always test your spinning line before each day's fishing. I don't know what causes nylon monofilament to lose strength, but it can and does, and the time to learn about it is *before* hooking a lunker, not *after!* Quite often, the last few feet of line will be noticeably weakened while the rest of the spool retains its full strength. You can save yourself much grief by discovering the weak section before setting out.

The number of different spinning lures, past and present, is almost astronomical, and no one fisherman could hope to test them all. I'm sure that all would take trout, given enough time and use, but only a few find their way to the top of the list by demonstrating their day-to-day superiority.

I have already named three Swiss lures—Long Spoon, Broad Spoon and Normal Spoon—as my personal favorites for general trout fishing. Also, I have named the Panther Martin as by far the best ultralight lure for use

Mooselook Wobbler   Dardevle Spinnie

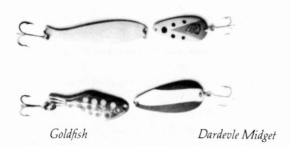

Goldfish   Dardevle Midget

Other time-tested spinning lures

on trout. More spinning lures which have proven their special worth to my satisfaction are: Dardevle Midget, Dardevle Spinnie, Al's Goldfish, the various Mepps spinner combinations in the smaller sizes and the Mooselook Wobbler in 1/6 oz.

Part of the fun of fishing is that of testing new lures, but I think I should warn against jumping to conclusions after only brief testing. Just as a fisherman can get lucky, almost any lure can get "hot" for a single day—but it may never again reach the same heights. It's the long run that counts, and most experienced fishermen come to count on a small number of proven lures, lures which have year after year produced for them best.

Finally we come to fly fishing, the one phase of trout fishing which is noted above all others for its lack of objectivity. Arguments arise regularly, but few are ever settled. As a result there are few absolutes to serve as standards of measure, and this is as true concerning individual tastes in fly rods as it is elsewhere.

I have done a fair amount of fishing in Maine, over quite a string of years. When I made my first trip my pet rod of the moment was an Orvis 7½-footer weighing less than 4 oz. (It's still going strong and is still a favorite.) Although the rod is light and exquisitely sensitive, it is tough, powerful and will toss all the fly line I have it in me to sling. Nevertheless, guides and local fishermen obviously regarded it as an affectation, a deliberate leave-taking of practicality. When asked to try it, they steadfastly refused to touch it on the grounds that they'd "prob'ly bust it."

These men had, as their cherished favorites, ponderous nine-foot rods which to me were heavy, lifeless and thoroughly unpleasant to use. The difference between these rods and mine was as obvious as the difference between an ungainly Rhode Island Red rooster and a trim fighting cock of half the weight, but those bound by tradition to long, cumbersome rods were blind to it.

Again, today's fly fishermen are lucky. Improvements in materials, engineering and craftsmanship have forced recognition of the fact that a fly rod's practicality is not a matter of length and weight. Depending on the type of fishing, "practicality" in modern fly rods begins at five feet, two ounces and seldom exceeds eight feet, five ounces. These light but powerful rods are a delight to use, a delight denied virtually to all fly fishermen but those of the recent past.

For centuries, rod makers depended on various woods as their only sources of material, none of which was satisfactory. There were lancewood rods still in use in my youngest days, and I cast flies and caught trout with at least one. It is still remembered as an abomination.

The bamboo rods of my youth weren't much better, at least those that I could afford to buy. All were long, heavy and soupy and utterly lacking in guts or backbone. I finally scraped together enough money to buy a fairly expensive rod, a 9-foot 5-oz. number which I treasured as a gem of perfection and which, by the standards of the time, it undoubtedly was. I still have it, and once in a while I joint it together and waggle it. It feels horrible, and I marvel at my one-time high opinion of anything so lacking in virtue.

Moreover, it cost me fully a week's pay. Yet it is vastly inferior to the Christmas-present rod, the cost of which represents little more than to-day's payment for two or three hours of common labor.

Although it is now possible to buy fly rods for only a few dollars which are better than the most expensive of a few decades ago, I do not recommend strict economy in fly rod purchases unless absolutely necessary. Fly casting is an art in which very small differences in fly rod design and action make big differences in degree of enjoyment. Each refinement of design and construction has its price, but if the money spent adds substantially to the pleasure of each day's fishing, it is my belief that it is well spent indeed.

When a really fine rod becomes the objective, the question of material arises, namely, glass or bamboo. Top-quality bamboo rods are more expensive than the best glass rods, and the angler must first decide whether he rates bamboo ahead of glass by way of performance and then, if so, whether he is willing to pay the difference in price for the difference in quality.

I can be of help in this matter only to this extent: Top-quality glass rods are fine rods indeed. In my opinion (count it for what you may), the best in glass doesn't *quite* equal the best in bamboo. To enjoy this small difference you must pay quite dearly, and while it is worth the price to me and other fishermen, as many more feel that it is a poor bargain. Each fisherman must make his own decision.

My experience with glass rods is rather limited so I am not qualified to make comparisons on the basis of actual experience. I can recommend only the "System" glass rods manufactured by Scientific Anglers, Inc., Midland, Michigan. The "System" concept (by the way, an innovation of this imaginative concern) consists of a series of rods and reels designed to handle lines of specific weight. A System Eight, for example, would include a rod scientifically engineered to handle an 8 line, a reel appropriate for the same line and the line itself, thus assuring the purchaser of a balanced outfit.

I have owned and used a System Six combination for several years, and have found the rod to be as advertised: light, stuffed with plenty of backbone and capable of laying out a long line with but little effort from the fisherman.

While I have not tested other glass fly rods thoroughly enough to comment on them, I can cite the results of a survey made by Eric Leiser of Melville, New York. Eric owns and operates a thriving fly-tiers supply business (Fireside Angler) and preparatory to adding a line of fly rods to his listings he polled his many mail-order customers as to their favorite brand of glass rods. The overwhelming choice was the Fenwick Feralite, so named because metal ferrules play no part in the rod's construction. It is interesting to note that this rod, probably the most popular glass rod in the world today, sells, in most weights, for around $35.00. This moderate price undoubtedly has something to do with the rod's popularity. Fly fishermen are a finicky lot, however, and I'm sure that they would not voice general acclaim for anything other than top performance and reliability.

System concept of Scientific Anglers, Inc. takes guesswork out of assembling a balanced outfit. Scientific Anglers, Inc.

Expert design, impeccable craftsmanship and impregnated bamboo make Orvis rods the first choice of many fishermen.
The Orvis Company, Inc.

When it comes to bamboo, I feel without reservation that Orvis rods of resin-impregnated bamboo are the best rods that money can buy. Orvis rods are carefully designed to provide a wide choice of actions over an equally wide range of weight and length, and the workmanship which goes into them is at every point superb. Yet this is only part of the story.

I own a substantial battery of Orvis rods, the oldest of which I have had for about 20 years. In two decades of hard and frequent use, this rod has refused to take a *set;* it is essentially as straight as it was a score of years ago. No amount of careful design or workmanship could have averted this affliction which is common to all other bamboo rods. (A "set" is a permanent curvature which develops with use.)

Such uncommon resiliency is achieved by impregnating the bamboo with resin by a patented process which has the effect of creating an entirely new material which is impervious to heat, cold, moisture and all but impervious to stress. In short, it is, in my opinion, the best rod-making material yet known.

Orvis rods are expensive, in terms of initial cost, but from long experience I can attest to their superb performance and almost incredible durability. Due to the long service they will give with reasonable care, their purchase as a first rod may prove to be an economy over the long haul.

With respect to length and action of a first fly rod, my choice would be a 7½ ft. rod of medium action, designed to handle a 6 weight line. This brings us to another important matter. The weight of the fly line supplies the inertia against which the fly rod can work to accomplish the cast. Obviously, rods of different power require lines of correspondingly different weights.

The standardization of fly line weights is a fairly recent blessing. Weights are now designated by number, beginning with 1 and running through 12. These numerical designations are accorded by virtue of the weight, in grains, of the first 30 feet of each line. The first 30 feet of a 1 weight line weigh approximately 60 grains; the corresponding section of a 2 weight line weighs approximately 80 grains, and so on to a 12 weight of approximately 380 grains per first 30 feet. Very few rods are designed to handle lines lighter than 3 weight, and those which take lines heavier than 8 or 9 weight are intended for Atlantic salmon fishing, steelhead fishing or salt-water use.

Fly lines also come in a variety of taper combinations and densities, which, at first glance, may make the matter of designation seem confusing. Let's walk through the various classifications step by step.

A level line is one of unvarying diameter throughout. Designation: L.

A double taper line tapers uniformly from each tip to a bulky midsection. Designation: DT.

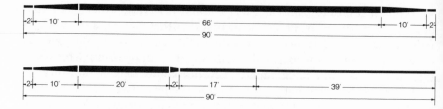

Double taper is best choice for most fly fishing. Weight forward taper is designed for extra long casts.
Scientific Anglers, Inc.

A forward taper tapers quite rapidly from the forward tip to a bulky "head" then back to a thin running line of constant diameter. Designation: WF (Weight forward).

Lines designed to float are allegedly constructed with a specific density of less than 1. Designation: F.

Lines designed to sink are constructed with a specific density of more than 1 (which apparently is easier to do!). Designation: S.

From these definitions, can we identify the following lines? (1) WF-7-F; (2) DT-6-S; (3) L-5-F. *Easy!*

      (1) Forward taper, weight seven, floating.

      (2) Double taper, weight six, sinking.

      (3) Level, weight 5, floating.

In the old days lines were classed by their diameters, the smallest diameter indicated by the letter H, then in reverse alphabetical order to the largest diameter A. An "HCH" line was a double taper of the indicated diameters. This was no help when it came to matching a line to a rod, for diameter designations were no indications of weight.

Rod manufacturers now simply recommend a particular line weight for each of their rods. This simplifies the matching process, for a rod designed to handle a 6 weight line, for example, will handle *any* line in that weight range regardless of its taper, diameter or density: WF-6-F, WF-6-S, DT-6-F, DT-6-S, L-6-F, L-6-S. Note that balance between rod and line is maintained through the various tapers, diameters and densities simply by staying in the 6 weight classification.

The double taper, floating fly line is undoubtedly the most popular and useful. Forward tapers are designed for maximum distance, and this need won't arise until later, if at all. Level lines are the cheapest and cast well. Their construction largely rules out any delicacy of presentation, however, so they are a poor choice.

While floating lines are especially designed for dry fly fishing, they are the most satisfactory for the beginner. Sinking lines are valuable at times, but they are difficult to cast since the line for the backcast must be retrieved from beneath the surface rather than from upon it. It would therefore be my advice to graduate to their use only after considerable experience with floating lines, regardless of whether you begin fishing wet flies or dry flies.

Floating or sinking, I think the choice of most experienced fly fishermen would be the famous Air Cel (floating) and Wet Cel (sinking) lines manufactured by Scientific Anglers, Inc. By specializing in the important field of fly line manufacture, this company has set what have become the modern standards for fly line excellence. I have used their lines for many years, and they have outperformed and outlasted all others—and in this case I *have* tested all the leading brands.

In selecting a fly reel the beginner may be distracted by ads pertaining to automatic or multiplying reels, but his most sensible choice for trout fishing is a single action reel. In a previous chapter I made it plain that the best bargain in single action reels is the Pflueger "Medalist," and that in some respects this reel is greatly superior to much more expensive reels.

Now, just to keep the game honest, I must admit that I'm a sucker for expensive fly reels, and own four English-made reels which set me back plenty. By nature I'm much more the slob than snob, but I have to confess to a certain pride of ownership pertaining to these reels which has nothing to do with any imagined superiority of performance. This means, of course, that I, like many others, have fallen victim to their snob appeal. Still striving for honesty, I can say that I really think I have my money's worth in terms of smug satisfaction of possession.

Such self-indulgence is easy to criticize from the sidelines, but just you wait! You may start out with a cold eye for practicality, but you won't get far before the indulgence bug bites you. Then, purely on impulse, you'll haul off and buy some expensive item of tackle or equipment which you don't really need and which you can't really afford. I'm more than a little inclined to believe that a certain amount of such self-indulgence always does a man's soul a world of good.

The fly fisherman is going to need flies, of course, and in his opinion he can never have too many. Standard patterns, alone, run into the hundreds, if not into the thousands, and new variations of these crop up regularly. In addition, creations which break with tradition are periodically hailed as the long-sought answer to the fly fisherman's problems.

At the moment, for instance, great claims are being made for dry flies that have been tied without hackle. Ever since the advent of dry fly fishing, followers of the art have pinned their faith on high-floating dry flies, flies which ride the surface jauntily on the very tips of choice, springy hackle fibers. "No good," declares this new school of thought. "Trout can't see the fly for all that bushy hackle. Get rid of it and give 'em a look at the body and wings."

Maybe so. Maybe, in only a few years, all dry flies will be tied without hackle, but I doubt it. The gates of tradition are stormed constantly, but major breakthroughs are very, very rare events.

Nevertheless, I, for one, could hardly wait to try this alleged panacea (with unimpressive results), and I'm quite sure that most dry fly fishermen, romanticists (suckers) all, reacted in much the same way. The point I'm trying to make here, however, is not that faddish innovations usually *fade* out rather than *pan* out, but that if a fellow follows his natural inclinations, he's going to need a lot of flies.

Excellent flies, of all types, sizes and patterns can be bought from an abundance of retail outlets as well as directly from professional fly-tiers. They are all the product of hand labor, however, and they must be expensive, from the fisherman's standpoint, if the hard working tier is even to make wages. The purchaser of average means thus finds himself sorely torn between two urges: that of economy which counsels minimum expenditure, and an even more powerful urge to possess, and carry on his person, twenty times the number of flies that he actually needs.

As a way out of this dilemma, virtually all of the serious fly fishermen of my acquaintance have learned to tie their own flies. Not only is it an economy measure, but it is a fascinating outlet for the modest amount of creativity allotted to most of us, and which otherwise might never see the light of day. Finally, and fortunately, it is an art which is not hard to master.

The best way to learn fly tying is to watch a competent tier at work. If that is not possible, one of the many fine instructional manuals which exist is next best. My top choice would be "Professional Fly Tying and Tackle Making," by George Leonard Herter. This is available from Herter's, Inc., Waseca, Minnesota. One in which all steps are made very clear by fine photographs is "Fly Tying," by Helen Shaw, available at bookstores and fly tying supply houses.

The necessary tools, plus materials from which hundreds of flies can be tied, can be bought for the cost of only a few dozen top-quality flies. Suppliers advertise regularly in all the outdoor magazines. One firm from which I have had excellent service is Fireside Angler, Box 823, Melville, New York.

Whether the trout fisherman uses bait, spin fishes or fly fishes, there are certain basic items that he will need. Choice of brand is seldom critical, so I shall merely point out the items themselves.

Unless you enjoy fumbling for slippery trout bare-handed, which I do not, a *landing net* is a must. Best means of carrying it is not from an elastic cord, but snapped to a ring which is tabbed to the back of your fishing jacket an inch or two below the nape of the neck. When not in use the net is handily out of the way, but can be flipped forward and unsnapped quickly whenever needed.

The *fishing vest* is an even greater necessity. It should have lots of pockets, large and small, inside and outside. Pockets should either be zippered or provided with snaps effecting tight closure so that items will not dribble out when the vest is tossed into the trunk of a car or elsewhere. It should be short, so that the contents will stay dry even during deep wading. Despite my declared intention of not naming brand names, I think the excellence of the Orvis Tac-L-Pak warrants an exception in this case. It has taken me nearly twenty years to wear out two of these excellently designed vests and I am currently working on a third.

Hip boots are adequate for wading small streams, but most rivers require the use of *waders.* To own less than both will put any trout fisherman at a serious disadvantage. *Felt soles* are a great help wherever stream bottoms are rocky and slippery, which is to say almost everywhere. Both boots and waders can be bought equipped with felt soles. Replacement kits are available, and the soles supplied in these can be applied to boots and waders with rubber soles as well as to replace original felts which have worn out.

A well equipped (stuffed) fishing vest will include the following: *insect repellant, dry fly floatant, line grease, flashlight, knife, scissors* or *clipper, leader pouch, spools of leader* and *tippet materials* in various diameters, and as many *fly boxes,* plastic or aluminum, as may be needed to carry your supply of *dry flies, wet flies, nymphs* and *streamers.* If you tend to stray from beaten trails, *matches* in a waterproof container and a *compass* are wise inclusions.

Trout fishermen certainly earn the right to keep a few trout for eating, and these should arrive home in the best possible condition. To accomplish this, I know of nothing as efficient as the old-fashioned wicker *creel* through which air can circulate and thus cool by evaporation. To guarantee the latter, carry a clean *sponge* in the creel and dip it in the stream from time to time when carrying fish.

Last, but almost most, comes overdue mention of the one item of equipment which, short of my last rod, reel and line, I would be most reluctant to part with: my *canoe!* I realize that a canoe is not for everybody, but for the eastern trout fisherman who has no aversion to this type of

craft, a canoe will broaden his trout fishing horizons as will no other single item of equipment. Bogs, beaver flowages, wilderness ponds, unwadable sections of streams and all other hard-to-get-at waters offer comparatively virginal fishing to the canoe owner.

I have made this plug for canoes many times before, but I do so once again without apology. I have owned a thirteen-foot Grumman lightweight for more years than I care to count, and much of my best trout fishing during this long span has been fishing that I could reach only with the little canoe's help.

To those who may consider buying such a craft, be advised that the secret of complete utility lies in holding down size and weight. I know that to many, thirteen-footer sounds like a risky compromise, but I can assure you that my fishing partners and I have found it nothing short of ideal for our trout fishing needs. The trouble with longer and heavier craft is that the labor involved in their transportation discourages their use—and they stay overhead in the garage. My lightweight weighs only 40 pounds; two fishermen can tote it almost anywhere with no sweat. As a consequence, it comes in for steady use throughout the fishing season. I usually take it atop the car on extended trips and have even flown to wilderness ponds with it roped to a pontoon. In my opinion, I can do no greater service to those who wish to make the most of the trout fishing potential than to recommend the purchase of a canoe.

This chapter has turned out to be lengthy, but only because the sum total of a trout fisherman's equipment is vital to his sport. If the explicity of my advice has exceeded the limits of my experience, as indeed it has, it is only because of the desire to help others acquire a rounded collection of gear which will serve them over the years as well as mine has served me.

A small, light canoe will open many new doors to good trout fishing.

The author's Grumman lightweight canoe has accompanied him on flights to wilderness ponds.

9

OF PLACES AND TIMES

If a fisherman were to devote his lifetime to fishing New England trout waters, I doubt very much that he could cover them all, let alone get to know them intimately. Merely fishing all the "Mud Ponds," "Round Ponds" and "Long Ponds" of Maine, New Hampshire and Vermont would be a considerable enterprise.

Quite unrealistically, eastern trout fishermen tend to think of New England's total trout fishing potential as one comprised only of well known waters: Battenkill, Kennebec, Androscoggin, Moosehead, Sebago, Allagash . . . Each in this category enjoys a well deserved reputation, but the list soon runs out and includes only a tiny fraction of all eastern trout waters.

How about Tinmouth Channel? Second Berry? Oliverian Stream? Probably not one fisherman in a thousand has heard of this trio of obscure trout waters, yet each furnishes interesting trout fishing in Vermont, Maine and New Hampshire, respectively. The counterparts of these minor streams and ponds total into the high thousands, and by far it is they which, collectively, provide the bulk of New England trout fishing.

It is a mistake to assume that to enjoy eastern trout fishing one must fish waters of widespread fame. In fact, hopes are often dashed by the competition which just this concept creates, whereas exploration of areas much less renowned, often lead to happier results.

As an example, I have lived for significant periods of time in several different locations in Vermont, the choice of each dictated by occupational necessity and with complete disregard for trout fishing opportunities. Yet I have enjoyed good to excellent trout fishing in each of these localities, with more good trout water in each than I could possibly tend to.

I cannot speak from experience concerning Connecticut, Massachusetts and Rhode Island, but I'm certain that it would be very difficult to hit on a location in Maine, New Hampshire or Vermont that offered no nearby trout fishing. Even in the highly urbanized states named above, I would risk a bet that there are more trout fishing opportunities than is generally suspected.

If I seem to be laying the groundwork for generalization, it is because it is the truth. As an outdoor writer, I have long since learned how risky, and even foolish, it is to offer well intended where-to-go advice to fishermen, and as a fisherman I have learned how foolish it is to try to follow the well intended advice of outdoor writers.

In the first place, editors of outdoor magazines take a dim view of tales in which the characters catch few fish, or none at all. In order to sell his output, the writer must write of action-packed days and spectacular catches. These are rare days in any fisherman's experience, but the wistful reader assumes that each is typical of the region about which it is written. Transported with excitement, he hastens to make reservation at the fisherman's paradise which the article has so clearly revealed. So do dozens of equally naive citizens.

In the meantime, the fishing camp that has been treated so glowingly, grateful for the rash of new business, invites the writer to return. Usually, the poor dope arrives simultaneously with the small army which his extravagant prose and pictures have attracted.

I speak from experience when I say that this can be very, very embarrassing for the outdoor writer. I have checked in at a fishing camp by invitation, to find every cabin jammed with guests who were there as the direct result of what I had written about the place. The greeting from each: "Where the hell are all those trout you wrote about?"

It's a touchy question. At least half the attracted guests will be indifferent trout fishermen at best, and the places in New England where tyros can take their limits of trout are virtually nonexistent. But there is more to it than that. The exceptional fishing which inspired the article is long a thing of the past. Perversity being what it is, the quality of the fishing will have sunk to an unprecedented low at precisely the time the camp fills with eager fishermen. I know, because I have gone through the whole painful routine on more than one occasion.

Therefore, in that which follows, I shall make no abortive attempts to steer the reader to places where the fishing is at all times exceptional. I shall refer to spots where I have been lucky enough to have had exceptional fishing, but my main pitch will be for the sum total of the New England trout fishing potential. Rather than try to name specific hotspots, real or imaginary, I would like to convince the reader that he can find interesting and worthwhile trout fishing almost anywhere he chooses to prospect in the three northern New England states.

If I were wilderness bent, and could shrug off the expense of a stay at a fishing camp and the cost of a guide, I would head for Maine in late May or early June. If I had to stretch my dollars, I'd explore the more accessible waters of New Hampshire or Vermont, any time from the first of June through September, June and September sharing first choice.

If I opted for independent exploration, my strategy would be to make my headquarters at a comfortable motel. From there, guided by common sense and information gleaned from local sources, I'd make daily forays to likely waters. I'm convinced that a fisherman could make out very nicely doing nothing more than that almost anywhere in Vermont or in the northern half of New Hampshire.

To be more specific, however, one spot which lies in the midst of more trout water than a man could fish in a month, is the vicinity of Newport in the northeast section of Vermont. Within about an hour's drive, or less, are Lake Memphremagog, Lake Willoughby, Seymour Lake, Big Averill Lake, Norton Lake, Salem Lake, Island Pond, Maidstone Lake and numerous small ponds. Each contains one or more of brook trout, rainbow trout, lake trout and landlocked salmon. In addition, there are the following trout streams: Willoughby River, Clyde River, Barton River, Missisquoi River, Nulhegan River, Connecticut River and many smaller feeder streams.

The Clyde River is a fine brook trout stream in its upper reaches, and holds browns and rainbows downstream from Salem Lake, through which it flows.

The Missisquoi is a brown trout stream.

All the other major streams hold rainbows, browns and a sprinkling of brook trout.

The smaller tributaries all cater to small brookies.

Several years ago I spent a week at a camp on Salem Lake. I remember one day during which I fished the Clyde River. During the morning I must have caught and released at least two dozen browns and rainbows in the section of river immediately below the lake. In the afternoon I fished the brook trout section in the vicinity of the town of Island Pond. There I caught an equal number of beautiful brookies, creeling enough for a memorable meal. All was dry fly fishing—and beautiful!

It was during this stay that I had my hair curled by what was probably the largest trout which I have ever laid eyes on in public waters. I had made the acquaintance of a young fisherman who claimed to have taken a large number of trout of 3 pounds or so from a pool beneath a dam on the Black

River in the tiny village of Irasburg. Excited by his tall tales, I arranged to meet him there one evening. The dam was the old-fashioned wooden variety; an incline of planks supported by a cribbing of logs which also provided impenetrable cover for any trout inhabiting the large pool below the dam. We fished the river with some success, taking a number of small rainbows and browns on dry flies. Then, as dusk closed in, my young companion announced that it was time to station ourselves alongside the big pool and await signs of trout activity.

The dusk deepened without bringing any show of action; I was about to declare that my presence had "put the whammy" on things as usual, when a form of incredible bulk shot to the center of the pool with the speed of a torpedo. The huge fish didn't break the surface, but it didn't need to to serve ample notice of its awesome presence; its displacement was so great that its underwater progress caused a bulge at the surface like the wake made by the passing of a horse mackerel.

The huge trout shot across the pool, circled and returned, all at jet speed. Reaching the center, for what purpose I know not, it churned the surface to instant suds with a mighty swirl—and then disappeared. We stood in shocked silence as the water calmed and peace returned to the pool.

During the display of might, I had instinctively made a cast toward the center of the commotion. As I retrieved my fly I reflected on the ridiculous futility of my puny effort. Had that leviathan deigned to grab my tiny dry fly on its tapered leader, I no more could have stopped him short of the log cribbing than I could have halted a freight train with the same equipment.

"I thought we were dealing with 20-inch fish," I said when I regained my faculties.

"There are some big fish in here," replied my young friend, thereby understating all previous understatements in the history of angling. That monster weighed a dozen pounds if it weighed an ounce! I can prove it by showing you what remains of the hair it caused to stand fully erect atop my head.

No, despite nightly attempts to lure that big trout with suitable tackle, it never again put in an appearance during my stay. But the point I'm making is that I encountered that huge fish, not while a guest in some famed fishing region, but in a village pool beneath a sawmill dam, of which I had never before heard or never before seen. Furthermore, in a week of independent prowling among waters which were largely unfamiliar, I caught many more trout, and enjoyed myself ever so much more, than I have done on more than one carefully planned trip to celebrated waters.

In writing this chapter it would have been easy to reiterate the information put out by the respective fish and game departments. This information can be helpful, but it can only hit the high spots. In the state of Maine, for example, there are 5,152 streams and 2,465 lakes and ponds, most of which are trout waters. Such a vast total cannot be dealt with so as to reveal a small number of opportunities that stand out clearly as "best." To be realistic, advice must paraphrase the old toper's response when asked to name a good brand of whiskey. "Hell," he declared emphatically, "they're *all* good!"

In New Hampshire and Vermont the story is much the same. A relatively small number of well known and hard fished waters are available, but a great number of streams, lakes and ponds of only local reputation steadily furnish fair to excellent trout fishing. Usually good prospectors can stumble on good fishing by exactly the type of exploration I recommend.

Until quite recently, Vermont's Otter Creek, in the vicinity of Middlebury, provided some of the best dry fly fishing for rainbows and browns that it has ever been my good fortune to enjoy. The food supply was so rich that fish which lived through three winters were 18-inchers weighing better than 2 pounds apiece.

Throughout most of its length, from Wallingford to Lake Champlain, Otter Creek is a sluggish stream, populated mainly by northern pike, smallmouth bass, yellow perch and the like. Only in rare stretches of fast water did trout such as I have described flourish, and these stretches never became generally known.

Each season, however, the same regulars haunted these rips. What may have been half were residents of other states who had lucked into the discovery of that wonderful fishing.

For years thereafter, until ecological changes removed the trout, their fishing vacations were simple and economical affairs: lodging at a nearby motel, meals in restaurants handy by, and no expenses for guides or boat rentals. For but trivial cost, and in water not even recognized as trout-holding by the Vermont Fish & Game Service, they enjoyed annually some of the best fly fishing to be found in all of New England.

Several years ago, my longtime friend, H. G. Tapply, moved from Massachusetts to Alton, New Hampshire, a small town which is bounded in part by the shoreline of huge Lake Winnepesaukee. Tap didn't make his move on the strength of the area's fame, if any, as a trout fishing center, but now, years later, his letters continue to include enthusiastic accounts, not only of newly discovered trout waters, but also of new waters which he has heard about but hasn't yet been able to check out. Standing in his way are such chores as fishing for landlocked salmon in Winnepesaukee itself, bugging smallmouths in nearby Lake Wentworth, tending to the largemouths and pickerel in Gilman Pond and other equally irksome and time-consuming tasks. Some people have it rough!

Somewhat enviously, I submit my friend's happy circumstance as further proof of my contention that it is harder to find troutless regions in New England than to find areas which afford good trout fishing.

As another area where I think prospecting would be particularly likely to bring high returns (no guarantee, mind you!), I would recommend the region drained by Vermont's White River. The White is a tributary of the Connecticut, joining the latter at White River Junction. The White River proper rises in the vicinity of Granville, some 40 miles from its mouth. Over this course its flow is augmented by four major tributaries, each a trout stream of substantial size: First Branch, Second Branch, Third Branch and Tweed River. All these have smaller tributaries, of course, as does the main river. Altogether, there exists a network comprised of many miles of trout water, all of which is easily reached and which is capable of producing fine trout fishing when conditions are favorable.

The fisherman who makes his headquarters in the vicinity of Bethel will be within easy driving reach of virtually all parts of this waterway. Downstream lies water which holds, and sometimes gives up, trophy-size browns and rainbows. (It also holds various warm water species which stray upstream from the Connecticut.) Rainbows and browns predominate in the four major tributaries, and in much of the upstream portion of the main river. These same streches hold a scattering of brookies, with the concentration increasing in the upstream direction. The small feeders cater mainly to small brook trout, although rainbows and browns sometimes move into them.

Years ago, shortly after I moved to my present home and knew virtually nothing about the local trout fishing possibilities, I set out on a particular Saturday afternoon, guided by nothing but the desire to explore. I crossed the Green Mountain Range, via the Brandon Gap, and after crossing, and deciding against, several small mountain streams, I finally reached the floor of the White River Valley in the vicinity of Rochester.

The river itself looked inviting, too small to be difficult but plenty large enough to be interesting. I decided to have a go at it.

Working upstream with a dry fly, I had one of the most satisfying afternoons of trout fishing that I have ever enjoyed. Not only did I find willing rainbows, browns and brook trout in almost every run and pool, but the thrill of each rise was enhanced by the elation of discovery.

The water of the White River is dramatically clear, and I still remember the curious way in which it foreshortened, and thus disguised, the true length of the fish I caught. I would hook what appeared to be only an eight- or nine-inch trout, only to have the rod buck and throb under what seemed completely disproportionate resistance. When finally scooped up in the net, each "nine-incher" would stand revealed as a foot-long (or thereabouts) trout.

Another Vermont location where a fisherman needs only his tackle, car and enough coin of the realm for lodging and meals, is the vicinity of Morrisville. Here the Lamoille River, that section between Hardwick and Jeffersonville, provides at least 25 miles of excellent potential. Once it attains substantial size, the Lamoille holds rainbows and browns, including sizable specimens of both species. In its upper reaches, as is true of most Vermont trout streams, it offers brook trout for the many who rate them as sentimental favorites.

Here, again, the stream is readily accessible throughout its entire stretch. It is fished, of course, and the trout are no pushovers. But they are there for those who can take them, and that is all that most serious trout fishermen ask.

All eastern trout fishermen should give the Battenkill a try, for it is a remarkable stream in more ways than one.

First, perhaps, is its ability to maintain a strong, cool flow during the hottest weather and despite the most severe droughts. As a result, it is, I believe, the one Vermont stream of major size still capable of supporting brook trout. Less endearing, perhaps, is its success in evolving strains of trout, brookies and browns, so wary as to be almost unassailable.

Outwardly, however, everything seems to favor the angler; long, easily waded flats where a dry fly can be floated with no visible trace of guile, plenty of fish rising during most days, and dozens showing come evening.

If they are Battenkill brookies, usually fish of only eight to ten inches, you tie on a No. 18 or smaller *and* if you are lucky, you may raise a few. If you are lucky enough to get a crack at a much larger brown on the feed, the chances are that you will put him down with your first cast.

Battenkill catches are therefore generally light, but most fly fishermen count it a worthwhile experience just to come up against what must be close to the ultimate in trout sophistication.

Although most of Vermont's portion of the Battenkill is wadable (the river enters New York state west of Arlington), there is a mile or so of stream which lies just upstream of Arlington which is too abruptly deep to wade and which can be fished satisfactorily only from a canoe. The state maintains a small launching area at its downstream end, in fact, but compared to the rest of the stream this exceptionally deep stretch is but lightly fished. I doubt that the trout therein are significantly less wary, but the solitude and comparative absence of competition seems to the fisherman to give him an advantage. Also, as a point of personal interest but small significance, I *have* managed to take a couple of browns of over three pounds from this section of the Battenkill, something which I have been unable to do elsewhere.

The foregoing have been but a few Vermont opportunities which can be explored without great cost or effort. There are many others, and I'm sure that New Hampshire has numerous counterparts.

I'm willing to bet, for example, that from a headquarters in or near Conway, in the area drained by the Saco River, a man could find rewarding fishing by prospecting on his own and by following up leads obtained locally.

Another possibility: The Baker River in the vicinity of Warren. I have fished this stream with good results, and I have lasting memories of some of its deep pools washed from solid granite. My experience wasn't conclusive, of course, but I'd be willing to gamble on it.

One New Hampshire stream that I *haven't* fished, but would like to, is the Androscoggin, downstream from the town of Errol. I have heard heady tales of wildly leaping rainbows, and even occasional landlocked salmon, from those who have fished it.

While in the vicinity I would make a determined effort to fish both Swift Diamond and Dead Diamond Rivers, for in the days of my youth I listened agog to tales of five pound brookies which came from these twin streams. I'm not naive enough to expect that such brookies still swim therein, but from what I have heard, the two rivers still furnish what must rank as good brook trout fishing by today's standards.

When it comes to Maine's trout fishing, I cannot recommend the same casual approach in good conscience. While I am sure that there are localities where a stranger could find good trout fishing by his own efforts, I suspect that these are relatively rare. In my own case, most of my Maine trout fishing has been done while a guest at fishing camps and with the help of guides, at least until I got to know the country, after a fashion.

Every eastern fisherman should pit his skill against Battenkill trout at least once.
The Orvis Company, Inc.

Only a few decades ago, much of northern Maine offered what was almost frontier fishing for brook trout. Two- and three-pound fish were quite common, with four- and five-pounders showing up with some regularity. Such happy conditions no longer prevail. Today, a Maine brook trout of two pounds is a bragging fish. Thirty years ago it wouldn't have rated a second look.

This is not to put down Maine trout fishing. On the contrary, Maine stands out more than ever as the one brook trout state in New England. It still produces brookies of substantial size from most of its trout waters, whereas about all that remain in the other New England states by way of brook trout are the pygmies of small mountain streams, or the output of hatcheries.

The difficulty for the visiting fisherman is not the scarcity of trout, but the character of Maine trout waters. With respect to streams, those of Maine, unlike those of New Hampshire and Vermont, do not flow through valleys which invite the construction of bordering roads. Instead, they flow through swamplands and bogs, terrain which discourages roadbuilding.

As a result, most Maine streams of interest to the trout fisherman traverse sections of wilderness and are thus not open to easy exploration. Almost invariably, the stranger needs the help of a guide and his equipment in order to reach them.

Equally difficult to reach in many cases are the wilderness ponds which make up a significant part, if not the bulk, of Maine brook trout fishing. Again, a guide and his canoe are vitally needed.

My partner, Pete Terwilliger, and I fished for quite a string of years in the Jackman region. This is drained by the Moose River, an excellent brook trout and landlocked salmon river in certain spots and over certain stretches. Apart from the river, the bulk of the fishing is furnished by some 200 ponds and lakes which dot the surrounding wilderness.

When I first fished in the region there were many ponds which could only be reached satisfactorily by plane. Access to others could be gained only by long hikes through the wilderness or by all but smashing a Jeep

A river canoe trip is one of the highlights of Maine trout fishing.
Maine Department of Inland Fisheries and Game

to smithereens over primitive trails. I remember a particularly bone-crushing ride to one lake, so jolting that on the return trip I insisted on walking. I also remember flying in to one remote pond which was so small that the pilot would fly only one fisherman at a time. Even at that, we barely cleared the tops of the spruces, coming and going. Needless to say, I enjoyed some fine fishing in those remote waters.

But in the relatively few years since, many good roads have been built by the lumber companies which own the land. These are open to fishermen, and the increased pressure quickly and drastically reduced the quality of the fishing.

This brings to attention an unfortunate characteristic of the brook trout: It will not stand up to fishing pressure as will the browns and rainbows of many hard fished streams. The problem in Maine, unlike that in Vermont and New Hampshire, is to get beyond the heavy competition. Thus, despite the increase in roads and accessibility, the Maine visitor needs a competent guide as much as ever and perhaps more.

Just as pitting one's skill against the sophisticated trout of hard fished eastern waters is a phase of trout fishing with its own inimitable charm and flavor, so is a fishing trip by canoe along a Maine wilderness waterway. To me, at least, the primitive connotations of canoes and portages, campfires and outdoor cooking, have the effect of satisfying what in me is the haunting desire to move backward in time. The cry of the loon, glimpses of deer, bear and moose and the taking of "native" trout help to complete the illusion.

In the Jackman Region, the Moose River "Bow Trip," previously referred to briefly, is a good example of the kind of trip I have in mind. It covers a reputed 65 miles of river, which a party can negotiate at any pace it chooses. It provides fishing for wild brook trout over the entire course, with many hot spots along the way to look forward to. Several easily reached outlying ponds make interesting diversions. Downstream from Holeb Falls, the fastest stretches of water are shared by both trout and landlocked salmon, doubling the possibilities and the anticipation.

Moose River, Allagash, Moosehead, Rangeley, Fish River, Kennebago, Penobscot, Kennebec, Chamberlain, Chesuncook—names rich in tradition, symbolizing the wilderness and, each in its turn, denoting a major river drainage or lake in Maine—thus a major trout and salmon fishery. Fishing camps are operated in all these and other areas, most of which are advertised regularly in the outdoor magazines. All provide what I have described as typical of Maine trout fishing: close-to-base fishing, certainly, but also trips to outlying wilderness ponds and streams and river trips of several days.

It would be ridiculous for me to attempt any rating or comparison of the many camps in the numerous areas. I can only voice my sincere conviction that the ingredients of good fishing and lasting memories exist at all of them. It is only a matter of getting there at the right time, a matter over which we have very little control as any seasoned fisherman has good reason to tell you.

The *right time* is a time when everything falls into place, temperature, weather, fish metabolism—the works. The *timing* of a trip is something else again. Here the fisherman can act to improve his chances, even though he may fall short of guaranteeing his success.

It is highly important to plan for any Maine trout fishing trip before hot weather sets in. Due to the brook trout's extreme intolerance of high temperature, most of Maine's trout ponds, and all but its coldest streams, tend to "go dead" about the first of July and don't come to life again until fall. The best fishing usually falls between May 15 and the end of June. Weather conditions being "normal," my top choice would be the first week in June. It must be understood, of course, that foul weather can ruin a trip despite the best of timing.

Unfortunately, the best fishing comes just when black flies are at their worst. In the Maine woods during June, these bloodthirsty demons will all but devour alive any fisherman who doesn't keep himself well anointed with repellent, so prepare accordingly.

As already indicated, the trout fishing in New Hampshire and Vermont is not so critically seasonal. Seasons open around the first of May, but conditions during the first several weeks are usually marked by water that is too high and temperatures that are too low for good fishing. June is usually the best fishing month, but the fishing holds up fairly well in most streams through July and August. Chances are best during early morning and during the evening. The best mid-day bid is usually a mountain stream where shade and springs tend to hold the water temperature down.

September should be given serious consideration. There is little competition, the air is cool and refreshing and the foliage is often a sight to behold. Best of all, the trout, particularly the larger ones, are likely to be on the feed, their appetites whetted by the cooler water. As a result, the September fisherman quite often totes home his biggest trout of the year.

Past generations of New Englanders took the presence of trout in their streams as much for granted as they took the presence of the water itself. Perhaps it has been mainly due to this complacency that I have seen the trout's hold on survival deteriorate until, today, it is tenuous at best.

Only by the thinnest of margins does trout fishing still exist, restricted in scope, compromised by the hatchery truck, but still fulfilling and sustaining to the many who are attuned to its unique delights. But like most natural blessings, in which light it is properly viewed, it must be utilized in moderation, and with restraint, if it is to endure.

It is my hope that this book will be of help to those who are drawn by Nature to the traditional New England sport of trout fishing. Above all, it is also my hope that within the hearts of trout fishing's new followers will develop a love and respect for this fragile and endangered boon, and *a determination to do all that lies within a fisherman's power to guarantee its survival.*